MARKETING

KARMA

Use Karma to position yourself as an expert in your industry, attract your perfect client automatically, and grow your business exponentially.

Jorge S. Olson

ISBN 978-1-945196-40-9

Manufactured in the USA

Edited and Produced by Cube17, Inc.

Cover by Jacqueline Gonzalez De Leon

-First Edition-

To all the dreamers and doers who believe in the power of kindness and unselfish promotion.

This book is for you.

Table of Contents

Introduction

Karma for the West

A Buddhist monk converses with his friend:

"How have you been, my old friend?" the monk asks. "I've been depressed these few days," replies the friend. "Why are you depressed?" asks the monk. "My life is not what I thought it would be," he says. "What did you want from life that you did not get?" asks the monk. "It's not so simple," the friend says. "I'm just not happy." "Are you always unhappy? Or just these few days?" the monk asks. "Just these few days. I was fine before that," says the friend. "Would you like me to make you perpetually happy?" asks the monk with a gentle smile. "Yes," the man sits up straight. "I would love that." "Very well. I will give you the old Buddhist secret formula," says the monk, leaning closer. The friend leans in eagerly to hear. "Starting today, you will work daily to make your wife, three daughters, mother, and father happy. We'll start with them for now," says the monk thoughtfully. "But how will that make me happy?" asks the friend. "Karma," says the monk.

Karma is cause and effect. It's not about doing good, meditating, or giving back. It's as simple as cause and effect. If you mistreat people, you're still practicing

Karma. But if your reason is bad, your effect will be bad, too. It will affect others negatively and eventually you.

Karma for the West or What I Call Unselfish Promotion

Karma is often portrayed as the above story involving Buddha or a Buddhist monk. For many, it's hard to adapt these concepts to daily life, work, business, or social interactions. Yet, we all have a powerful urge to survive, be loved, be accepted, and succeed. Instead of trampling over others to achieve our goals, we can take a different approach towards ultimate happiness—Unselfish Promotion. This path is easy to understand, but committing to it might require unlearning decades of self-centered survival tactics.

Imagine applying the monk's story to business. You're with your mentor, a successful entrepreneur. You tell your mentor you haven't achieved the success you want. You're not the CEO, not earning as much as you want, and you're not happy. Your mentor tells you to make your employees happy, from salespeople to customer service reps and even strangers. "This will make you rich," he says. He tells you to smile at everyone and ensure people are always comfortable and happy around you. When you ask how this will make you happy, he replies, "Karma, Unselfish Promotion."

Marketing Karma isn't just about gaining power, followers, promotions, or personal branding. It's about how the world sees you and how you see the world. If you see the world in black and white, that's what you project. If you're all about money and power, that will be your legacy, and you'll attract or repel similar people.

Imagine your internal energy as a color. Everything you believe, carry, fear, and love is painted in this color. Marketing Karma is about projecting this color, your internal energy, and sharing it with others—starting with your family, then friends, then at work or business, and finally with the world using modern marketing tools.

How Does Marketing Karma Work?

Let's use an example: If you make your kids, colleagues, and friends feel loved and important, the universe will conspire to make you feel important, loved, and happy. You might be thinking, "I lost you at the 'the universe will conspire' part." Don't worry; it's more straightforward and logical than any metaphysical formula. It's about social anthropology. When you make others feel important and loved, they have a biological reaction— releasing happy hormones like serotonin and endorphins. Over time, people want to be around you, reciprocate your politeness, and feel good themselves. It's the science of Karma!

This book isn't entirely about meditation or mindfulness, but it's impossible to communicate who you are without knowing what's in you. This includes your energy, color, feelings, and thoughts.

What Is Your Energy?

What is your Karma? Your Chi? Your Unselfishness? What are your feelings about life, love, money, and family? What do you feel when you pick up a baby, especially your baby? That energy, that tingling sensation, is what we need to find and communicate without words. Everyone who sees you—your kids, spouse, friends, colleagues—should know how you feel and who you are.

Discovering Your Essence

This book is about finding your essence and communicating it to others without words.

This is the second edition, and it feels like a different book. It has grown with my experiences, interactions, relationships, meditation, and study. The first edition was written in thirty days, goal-oriented, with practical advice on self-promotion at a personal level within the family and in business. It covered building and extending your personal brand to your job and company.

This edition has more. It explores and discovers who you are and what you stand for. If you're unsure, we'll explore it together. This is crucial because to communicate effectively, you need a clear message. If the message is you, we must first understand who you are.

This exploration will lead to an inevitable question: What makes you happy? Without knowing this, it isn't easy to establish goals. After all, happiness is likely the most crucial goal. If you're happy, everything else is secondary.

Your goal for this book is to understand Marketing Karma, use it in your personal life, and grow your business with it.

First, we'll define Marketing Karma and its significance. Then, we'll illustrate how to apply it across different aspects of your life (business, personal, political, nonprofit, etc.). Finally, you'll learn advanced strategies for self-promotion using Public Relations, Social Media, Internet Marketing, Publishing, and other effective techniques.

You Aren't a Natural-Born Leader

You reach Marketing Karma when people follow you because they know you'll do the best for them, and they're better off with you than without you. Marketing Karma isn't about power or control; it's about detaching yourself from the need to give orders or even speak. How can this be possible? Marketing Karma is the absence of power. It's acting in the best interest of your team, employees, or family. This unselfish behavior sets your Marketing Karma in motion, making people naturally follow you.

Are you a natural-born leader? You don't need to be. Marketing Karma aims to transform you into a leader with magnetism and influence through your example.

Some leaders are naturally magnetic, inheriting their personality from their genetic pool. But this is only one-third of what you need to achieve Marketing Karma. The term "magnetic leader" comes from history and social anthropology, describing charismatic leaders or chieftains who reached their positions through their personalities.

The Influence Machine

It's essential to understand the role of Karma in leadership, marketing, and life. Without this understanding, you won't fully benefit from the mind shift of marketing karma.

After reading this book, you'll recognize your influence on those around you and how to use that impact through Marketing Karma. You'll learn modern interpersonal communication techniques with family, friends, and colleagues, and how to extend your message across ages and borders using mass communication strategies.

Your Brand Management Guide

Consider this book a guide to Brand Management for your Personal Brand. You are your brand manager, responsible for protecting and growing your brand. Everything you do reflects on your brand. People will equate you with your brand, sharing the same energy and purpose.

When I first purchased my house, I needed to clean the bathtub. Covered in hard water stains, I tried everything with no luck. Frustrated, I went to Home Depot. There, a merchandising manager for a cleaning product approached me. He was tall, fit, and clean-cut, wearing a well-ironed blue polo shirt with a yellow Zep logo. He listened to my dilemma, selected a product, and assured me I could return it if it didn't work.

This experience was made not by the brand but by the person. This is why learning Personal Branding is essential. Even if you're the CEO or CMO of a Fortune 500 company, you need to establish a personal branding culture. Your employees are your company's face, mouth, ears, and experience. All of this starts with you. If you can't sell yourself, you won't be able to sell a product, service, or belief.

Conclusion

You are your own Brand Manager. Communicate your best value proposition and convince others why you are great. Your magnetic personality might suffice with your immediate circle, but to reach the masses, you'll need modern communication tools like Public Relations, Social Media, and candid conversation. This book will teach you easy and advanced marketing techniques to promote yourself. The catch? You must do it all unselfishly, using Karma. Keep reading to discover how.

Mastering Marketing Karma

3 Learn Advanced Strategies

Explore advanced self-promotion techniques using various media.

2 Apply Across Life Aspects

Implement Marketing Karma in business, personal, and nonprofit areas.

1 Understand Marketing Karma

Grasp the foundational concept and its importance.

Figure 1- Mastering Marketing Karma

Chapter 1
What Is Marketing Karma?

This book is about marketing. That's no secret. But the real secret lies in how you'll use this newfound knowledge to market yourself, your products, your company, and your ideas for the rest of your life.

Yes, you heard that right—forever. Whether you're an executive, entrepreneur, raising capital, selling services, or involved in any business venture, these strategies will serve you well. Even if you decide to step away from owning a business, these strategies can help you land positions on boards of directors, secure investments, or even influence voters if you run for office.

The know-how, strategies, and techniques you'll learn here will create powerful neural connections in your brain. Why is this important? Because these connections will turn you into a marketing superstar. Soon, you won't even have to try. Your brain will be hardwired to apply Marketing Karma in every situation, not just in business, but in life.

Marketing Karma will transform your personal and business relationships. It will make you happy, aware, attractive, and influential. And yes, I said attractive. I don't mean just physically appealing—though that's a bonus—but you'll attract the people you want to attract. People will gravitate towards you, drawn by an unseen force. You won't just have a magnetic personality; you'll have an electromagnetic force as strong as the forces binding atoms and molecules.

Behold the Secrets of Marketing Karma

Marketing Karma might seem like a mystical secret accessible only to the enlightened, those who can recognize the hopes and dreams of everyone they meet. But in reality, Marketing Karma is not a mythical power. It's a formula that yields measurable, repeatable results in your life and business. Yes, it can make you money, but it can also make you happy.

The formula is simple: Marketing Karma = Unselfish Promotion.

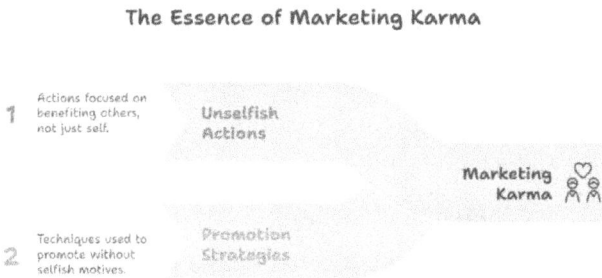

The Essence of Marketing Karma

1. Actions focused on benefiting others, not just self. — Unselfish Actions

Marketing Karma

2. Techniques used to promote without selfish motives. — Promotion Strategies

Figure 2 - The Essence of Marketing Karma

Marketing Karma in the East translates to Unselfish Promotion in the West. No, unselfishness and promotion are not oxymorons. They're the path to achieving your life, business, and family dreams. Even better, it will make everyone in your circle happier. If you don't care about their happiness, that's the first part of the formula we need to fix.

Understanding Marketing and Karma

To grasp Marketing Karma, we first need to understand what marketing and Karma are. Many people think marketing is simply about making money or selling a product. The short definition of marketing is the act of promoting and selling a product or service. This is a great starting point, but it's both too general and too specific.

Let me explain. This definition works well for traditional businesses. It involves influencing the market to create, promote, distribute, and sell a product or service. I learned this in college, used it as a VP of marketing for several companies, and taught it to thousands of clients. Traditional marketing involves market research, finding the perfect clients, designing, prototyping, producing, importing, warehousing, distributing, getting the product into stores, merchandising, advertising to the end user, and ensuring the product sells.

Modern marketing, however, goes beyond traditional methods and incorporates social media and other one-to-many promotional tools. Now, you can use print-on-demand publishing, LinkedIn, Twitter, Instagram, YouTube, Facebook, and blogs to promote your beliefs, religion, or even a political campaign. Getting a plug in a major magazine, newspaper, or viral video lesson on YouTube can create significant influence. Modern marketing is all about influence. Marketing Karma adds unselfish influence to the equation.

Traditional Marketing vs. Marketing Karma

Traditional Marketing Example: Wholesale Distribution

After my career in the software industry, I wanted to become an entrepreneur. I had been a CEO and VP at software companies but knew nothing about wholesale distribution or product development. So, I read the classifieds in the San Diego Union-Tribune daily until I found a small wholesale distribution business in San Diego. I applied my best practices and management skills and could afford it. Bingo!

I became the proud owner of a small distribution company that sold impulse items to convenience stores and liquor stores. That same year, I got married, paid for my wedding and honeymoon, and put a down payment on a home. I bet my life savings on this business, and my wife and I left the executive world for the life of entrepreneurs.

On day one, my wife and I had no savings, income, or idea of how to run a wholesale distribution company. We arrived at the warehouse at seven-thirty in the morning to start working. We hired the previous salesperson to help with the accounts, and the former owner agreed to assist us for two weeks.

After those two weeks, I made an impression on the former owner, Marshall Shields. He came out of retirement and invited me to create a new company focused on product development. We developed products and sold them to other distributors and major retailers, covering small independent stores and large chains. I created over a thousand consumer packaged goods from scratch, including beverages, vitamins, tools, pet supplies, apparel, electronics, home accessories, kitchen gadgets, sunglasses, and watches.

Traditional marketing methods were used: trade shows, samples in the mail, and cold calls. We sold directly to large accounts like Walgreens and Target and used distributors for other accounts. We used an impulse buy model with our racks, displays, and signage. Our best products sold for only $1.98 each. But we didn't use Marketing Karma until I did.

Marketing Karma Example: Wholesale Distribution

One morning, we lost a large chain and distributor simultaneously, significantly impacting our income. I decided we needed more distributors, especially smaller ones that paid cash. It was time to turn on the Marketing Karma machine.

I started a blog and a newsletter on how anyone could become a wholesale distributor. I held free conference calls, sent free information, and wrote articles and white papers. I invited people to train with my sales team in San Diego. Some had lost their jobs, others wanted to start a family business, and many just wanted extra income.

It worked. I grew my database to forty thousand subscribers. Thousands listened to my conference calls and audios, and many started their own businesses. As a result, our business reached its goal of becoming a national distribution network. Personally, it allowed me to sell my stake in the business and work part-time mentoring new entrepreneurs. I still mentor entrepreneurs today and host free webinars, podcasts, and other programs.

This example shows how to use Marketing Karma in business-to-business settings and connect with consumers and end users. You have to learn to promote yourself first. If you can't promote yourself, you can't promote anything else.

Building a National Distribution Network

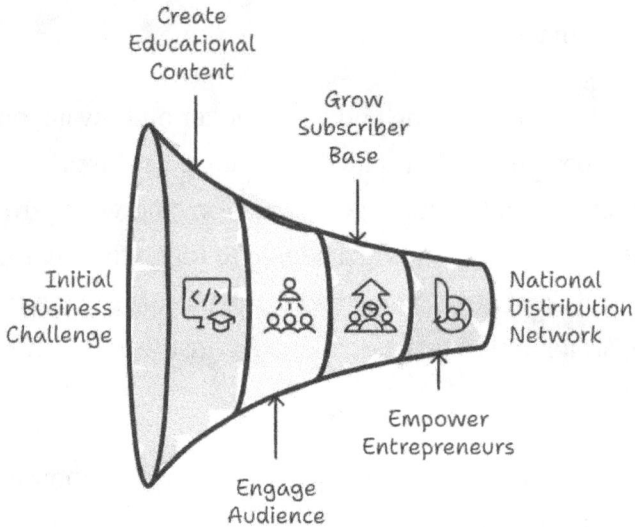

Create
Educational
Content

Grow
Subscriber
Base

Initial
Business
Challenge

National
Distribution
Network

Empower
Entrepreneurs

Engage
Audience

Figure 3 - Building a National Distribution Network

Back to Karma

In the previous example, I launched my search for distributors with value, information, and mentoring, not an ad. This positioned me as an expert and attracted a large following because I shared all the secrets. When entrepreneurs needed to buy products, they trusted me with their money. This unselfish approach built trust, expertise, and a loyal tribe.

Where Does Karma Come From?

The word Karma comes from India and is used in religions like Hinduism and Buddhism. It's a powerful, life-changing concept. It determines your happiness or misery, your suffering or your joy. The catch is that Karma is delayed. It affects your next life, not your current one- or does it? Karma is delayed, so we sometimes say "Instant Karma" when immediate results occur. The "next life" part of Karma can also mean your new, changed life, your new brain that expanded and grew. We'll dive deeper into the meaning of Karma, the 12 Laws of Karma, and Marketing Karma in the following chapters.

Karma means action. The actions you take are based on the actions you've received. If you experienced hate and cruelty, your Karma is of hate. You will express it and continue to receive it. It's your normal, your action, your Karma.

To change your future and your personal and business success, you need to change your Karma. Change is work, but it's the most remarkable thing in the universe. Change means growth. Think of everything in life that is stagnant versus everything that changes. Stagnant water is undrinkable, stagnant animals become fat, and if the earth stops, we all die. Change is growth.

When we continue to act the same way, we are stagnant. We treat colleagues, family, friends, employees, customers, and strangers similarly. At a business networking event, you introduce yourself, shake hands, ask what they do, hand them your business card, and see what benefit they can bring you. Sounds familiar?

We're just accepting the Karma we inherited. During your day, you don't think about Karma. You don't think about how the person walking by you feels, their life, or their family. You don't send good intentions with a prayer, meditation, or even a smile. But a smile can change your Karma in five seconds. It changes you immediately and the Karma of the person receiving your smile. Try it for one day. Concentrate on smiling at every human being you encounter. You'll see results. You'll wipe frowns from faces like a magic eraser. You'll get double-takes followed by smiles. People will wonder why you're so happy.

Happy Karma

Small changes in your Karma will reward you with significant successes in your relationships, business, life, and happiness. Karma covers happiness, not just in the next life, but in this life. Those who can change their Karma can accelerate their happiness instead of waiting for transformation over many lifetimes.

Changing your Karma into Marketing Karma could take some work and reprogramming your neural connections. Luckily, this won't take years. The techniques you'll learn here work like software. You just need an upgrade. This upgrade will give you a new perspective on life and business. It will transform your personality into an electromagnetic marketing machine capable of attracting business at a molecular level.

What Are You Promoting?

I was never the most popular kid in high school. I didn't join any particular group but had different groups of friends. I wasn't interested in belonging to one group or another or having a set group of friends. I wasn't a complete loner. I played sports, made varsity every year, and participated in social service school groups. My meditative demeanor was influenced by being an only child. I spent much time alone as my mother and grandmother worked all day. Looking back, I realize my social intelligence wasn't fully developed, and I thought I was above belonging to a group. I was wrong.

In my teens, I thought my colleagues were immature. I had friends but spent a lot of time alone, which gave me time to think. Looking back, I see my social theories were incorrect. Many of my friends are still immature, but I've changed. Now, I have fun with them, accept them, and appreciate their personalities.

As an only child, I never had to compete for attention. I was the firstborn of my entire extended family. I didn't realize you had to compete for attention until I was a teenager. Since then, I've seen how others fight for attention from their parents, teachers, friends, and, later, the opposite sex. This competition stays with you through life as you need to compete for jobs, business, sales, or simply to voice your opinion.

I've fought for attention in business, starting as a part-time employee wanting more hours than wanting to earn more per hour. As a software VP of marketing and business development, I fought for attention to get promotions and sell software. As an entrepreneur, I had to get the attention of investors, clients, and employees. Even as a writer, I have to attract people interested in my ideas so they'll read my books.

What Are You Really Promoting?

What are you promoting? You're likely promoting much more than you think. Maybe you're promoting your business, a product, or a service. Perhaps you're promoting your ideas or stories in a book. Even if you're not in business, you promote your lifestyle, religion, and ethics to your kids, extended family, and friends. At the very least, you're promoting to your teenagers, "Don't use drugs and stay in school."

Stop and think. It's essential to examine what you're really promoting when you promote your company, services, or products. Your business is important to you because it's yours. Your ideas are important because they're yours. So, what you're promoting is yourself.

You are the most important person you know, and people relate to people. People will always relate more to another person, especially one they like, than to any object, such as a product, service, or business.

What Is Self-Promotion?

Many of you will think, "Yes, I want to use self-promotion. I want to market and sell myself." Others will equate self-promotion with wanting all the attention or stealing it, seeing it as harmful. Before you decide, let's look at the definition of self-promotion in modern culture and our interpretation of it as Marketing Karma or Karma for the West.

According to Webster's Dictionary, promotion is:

1. The act or fact of being raised in position or rank.
2. The act of furthering the growth or development of something, especially the acceptance and sale of

merchandise through advertising, publicity, or discounting.

Now let's look at the definition of self:

1. The person that someone usually or truly is.
2. A particular part of your personality or character shown in a specific situation.
3. The personality or character that makes a person different from others.

You could devote your entire life to studying the self and write numerous essays from various philosophical perspectives. I've spent considerable time exploring this from practical and philosophical angles. However, for our purposes, we'll take a pragmatic view. You are the self. The real you—not the pretend you, the executive, the boss, or the star pupil. It's the real you, the one only you know, the one with insecurities who craves attention and acceptance. That's the person we need to know.

Remember, Marketing Karma = Unselfish Promotion. In reality, Marketing Karma equals Unselfish Self-Promotion. Adding "self" to the equation significantly impacts you because you need to change your view of promotion. Start with you, not your logo, product, service, features, or benefits.

Definition of Self-Promotion

- Grow, discover who you are, and share it.

- Show or share who you really are.

The concept of self-promotion may seem simple in theory, but it is complex in practice. It urges us to find ourselves, become better people, and share the new you with the world. Discovering who you are can take a lifetime. Growing and improving yourself might take several lifetimes, and learning to share or promote it could take another. Maybe we should reconsider reincarnation!

Always Be Transparent, Never Be Invisible

Show who you really are! Easier said than done, right? We spend so much time crafting our identities that we often start believing in them ourselves. When I was younger, a friend shared his "asking out speech" with me. He'd tell women he had money, drove an unaffordable car, and created a dating persona. This wasn't exclusive to men; a female friend had a "date speech" to present a version of herself she wanted her date to believe. I always found that amusing.

You probably have a speech for yourself, your product, or your business. When someone asks, "What do you do?" what's your response? Is your pitch personal or robotic? Do you cover all the features and benefits or ask questions? Do you have a "work shield" around you, separating your professional and personal selves?

Don't fear transparency. Let everyone see you, even at your worst—when you're worried, sad, or insecure. Likewise, learn to be happy at all times and show it.

What's the one thing you don't want to show or want to change? Anger. Get the anger out of your personality; never get mad. It's something you can avoid, so avoid it. Notice I said, "Don't be mad" instead of "Don't get mad." Anger is a state of being. You don't get it; you don't give it. People don't make you mad; you manage that on your own.

Enough philosophy; let's jump to the practical. What will you learn about self-promotion? You'll learn active and passive ways to catapult yourself to the front of every line and the top of every list by promoting, marketing, and selling yourself.

You will learn to sell, market, and promote your products and company, but not in the traditional, self-indulgent way. Instead, it will be done unselfishly.

I wasn't born a natural socialite, public relations guru, or self-promoter. I was never class president, football team captain, prom king, or the most popular kid. You don't have to be either. The concepts and strategies you'll discover here work even if you're an introvert. They have nothing to do with being outgoing or social. Remember, karma changes from the inside, not from the outside.

You'll appreciate the concept of Marketing Karma as if it were Unselfish Self-Promotion, as I once did. The difference is that I'm presenting all my years of observation, reading, studying, and experience in a concise, easy-to-learn, digestible form.

You won't have to change who you are or your social tendencies. Instead, you will reveal who you really are. In doing so, you'll realize how many people didn't know certain aspects of your life, and you'll see how many more people will be interested in you. This can include your family, boss, colleagues, customers, investors, friends, and anyone else you want to attract.

Why Unselfish?

Marketing Karma shows you how to promote yourself and be your own Brand Manager in business, personal life, politics, or charity work. Karma doesn't distinguish between your personal and professional lives. You either push good karma or you don't. If you're ruthless with your employees but loving with your family, Karma doesn't say, "It's okay; look at his family life." It just notices you're ruthless. This doesn't mean you'll have lousy karma only at work; it could affect your entire life.

The reverse could also be true. Perhaps you're too nice as a boss or entrepreneur, and people take advantage of you. Meanwhile, your home life is perfect. Is this a coincidence or Karma?

Why is Marketing Karma equal to Unselfish Promotion? It's unselfish because it teaches you to promote yourself for who you are without being flashy, ostentatious, or self-indulgent. You promote yourself by being unselfish.

The power of promoting yourself "unselfishly" is immense, and you'll be an expert by the time you finish this book. I know you have questions about how we'll do this. Everything will be outlined as we proceed.

The Unselfish Part of Self-Promotion

Did Galileo Galilei break your heart?

In 1613, Galileo, an Italian philosopher and astronomer, proposed a radical theory that got him arrested and excommunicated. His blasphemous idea shook the foundations of humanity. He claimed we're not the center of the universe. Sorry if Galileo broke your heart! In 1609, Galileo turned his newly invented telescope, an improvement on the Dutch spyglass, to the skies. It magnified stellar objects twenty times.

Galileo disturbed the status quo by supporting Copernicanism—the belief that the sun doesn't revolve around the earth. He sought to prove the theory proposed by Nicolaus Copernicus in 1543, which stated that we're not the center of the Solar System. This was hard to accept because religion taught that humans were the center of the universe by God's design. Denying this meant opposing God and the Church. Off with his head! No, not really. Galileo didn't lose his head. He died an older man, still working on science.

Karma Is Not a Piggy Bank

Don't use Karma expecting something in return. There's no "Karma meter." Karma isn't a piggy bank where good deeds guarantee rewards.

Being unselfish and marketing karma isn't new in business or politics, especially among seasoned salespeople. In sales, you're taught to put the customer first. This is an excellent example of unselfish promotion, though often it's not done correctly, becoming just another overused phrase like "value-added" or "the customer is always right."

An unselfish promoter places everyone first—family, customers, colleagues, charities, and strangers. Why? Because, like you, everyone has needs, wants, and problems. People think about these constantly, sometimes like a broken record.

These needs, wants, and problems vary, but everyone has them. Understanding this is half the work;

acting on it is the other half—the better half! This is why your promotion is unselfish. You know, everyone has dreams, aspirations, desires, needs, problems, and goals. They constantly seek advice, solutions, help, and comfort. This applies to all aspects of life, not just business or family. Being unselfish means recognizing that other people's thoughts are more important to them than to you. Respect and consider them.

Let's be the exception. Let's look at the world from others' perspectives. Focus on their needs, wants, and problems. Ask people about their lives, dreams, and needs. See how they open up, accept you, and appreciate you. People like those who are similar to them and those interested in them.

Marketing Karma First Step

Understand that everyone is just like you. Others have needs, wants, fears, and problems. Their thoughts are the most important to them and should be important to you, too.

Problem-Solving Mindset

Mindset is essential in marketing, especially in marketing karma, and it also applies to all aspects of business and life. We dwell on problems because they need fixing. If you can't fix it, it's not a problem; it's a fact. Our brains are wired to solve, to fix, to find solutions. Once a problem is solved, the brain moves on to the next issue. The challenge is to train your brain to stop fixating on imperfections and focus on what's right. This shift can change your state of mind, your attitude, and even your physical state. It works the other way around, too—change your physical state, and your emotions will follow. So, don't pout; stand tall and flash that smile. It's always tough to fake being happy, so your brain will eventually catch up.

Another strategy is to focus on good problems instead of stressful ones. If you don't have sound problems, find them. For example, I often have business problems. I've been involved with several publicly traded companies, funded numerous projects, and worked with over a hundred entrepreneurs. I've had my share of issues with investors, employees, customers, and everything that comes with being a serial entrepreneur. Usually, I don't take problems home, but occasionally, something or someone breaks a mental plate: maybe a rude customer or a meeting with a screaming vendor.

I use the good problem strategy to snap out of it. In my case, I might focus on writing—on a challenging idea or concept, if it's non-fiction, or on a character or storyline for fiction. Other people might turn to puzzles, redirecting their brains to fix the puzzle instead of their different problems. The idea is the same. Focus on something you enjoy that requires thinking and problem-solving. Your brain will more readily tackle a good problem than a bad one, and your emotions will be much happier.

The Cycle of Marketing Karma

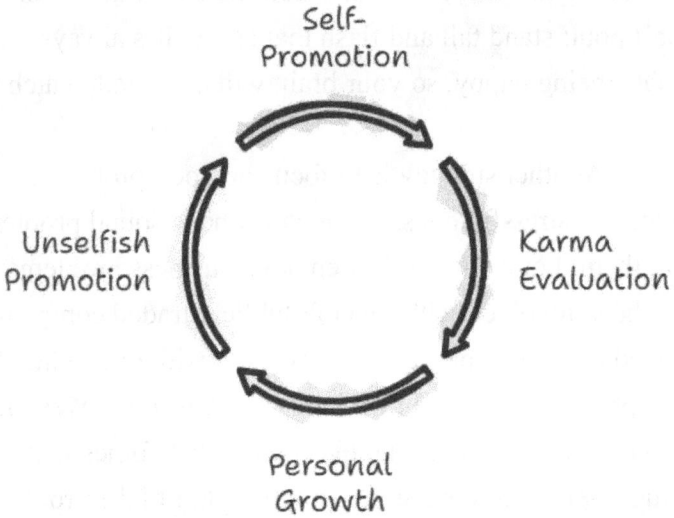

Self-
Promotion

Karma
Evaluation

Personal
Growth

Unselfish
Promotion

Figure 4 - The Cycle of Marketing Karma

Chapter 2
How I Discovered
Marketing Karma

I didn't learn Marketing Karma all at once; I discovered it by accident over many years of living and learning. It began at home with my mother and family, continued through school, and evolved with my work experiences and friendships. Don't worry; I won't recount a lifetime of lessons year by year. Instead, I'll share how I uncovered the secrets and methodology of Marketing Karma, influence, and self-promotion. You'll get what works—the hacks.

I first learned about Marketing Karma as a child from my mother and later at a private Catholic school, where the focus was on "helping by doing." It wasn't enough to set a good example; you had to take action. I didn't realize then that these lessons would transform into tools for promotion, attraction, influence, happiness, and even money. Later, I discovered other philosophies and approaches to Marketing Karma, including Hinduism and Buddhism from the East and Western philosophies from Aristotle and Plato to Saint Thomas Aquinas. But it wasn't all philosophy or religion. Marketing Karma is not just mysticism; it's rooted in history, psychology, and anthropology. After all, influence is based on motivation. What motivates your prospect to act, make a decision, or buy?

Experiences also shaped every strategy in Marketing Karma. My childhood visits to orphanages with my mother are a prime example. Despite having little money ourselves, my mother believed money had nothing to do with charity or Karma. She collected food and clothes from family and friends to take to underprivileged orphanages. These visits became normal activities, as routine as going to school. I thought everyone did this. I was wrong.

As a teenager, I was athletic and passionate about sports, especially basketball. I was also deeply involved in social work through a religious apostolic group at my school. We would visit impoverished neighborhoods in Tijuana on weekends—places without water, electricity, or roads. People lived in cardboard shacks with dirt floors.

Tijuana Hustle

Ten to twenty of us would walk two miles through undeveloped hills to these neighborhoods every week. We warned newcomers about the risks and necessary precautions. Our tasks included social work, religious work, and rehabilitation. We built roofs, houses, and schools, registered new kids for school, and helped with city documentation. The religious work involved baptisms, first communions, marriages, and spiritual guidance. Rehabilitation was the hardest, trying to motivate heavy drug users to take action. What could motivate them more than drugs? Their parents? Their kids? A goal? A dream? God? This was the most challenging and disheartening part of our work.

One summer day, we made our rounds through the neighborhood. It was hot, dry, and dusty. As cars passed, they kicked up clouds of fine dust that stuck to your skin and got in your eyes and mouth. I remember wiping my lips and grinding my teeth against the dirt.

Walking up the hill, I left my friends behind at various locations. I went to a small cardboard shack where an 85-year-old woman I liked to visit lived.

"Excuse me," I heard a faint voice. I turned towards it.

"Are you Jorge?" a woman asked, standing outside her home.

"Yes, ma'am, I'm Jorge," I replied, wondering how she knew my name.

"Your friends told me about you. They said you might help my son," she said.

I walked over and shook her hand. "Hi, I'm Jorge. What can I do for you?"

She was wearing an old dress, clean but weathered. Her eyes looked worn and tired, devoid of hope. "My name is Maria Estrada," she said. "Your friends work with the children. I thought maybe they could help my son, too."

"What's wrong with your son?" I asked.

"He's on drugs," she said, tears streaming down her face. "He's been using for two years, but for the past year, he does nothing but use drugs. He gets lost for days, steals, lies, sleeps all day."

"Where is he now?" I asked.

"He's home today. That's why I thought you could help him," she replied.

I took a deep breath. "What can I possibly do?" I thought. I had no training, no experience, no knowledge. "Yes, I'll help," I said.

Maria went inside and brought out a young man. "Talk to him," she said, her voice firm and accusatory.

"Not the best introduction," I thought.

The young man, about 25 years old, stood there shirtless, wearing only dirty jeans and a coat of crusty dirt. His hair was short and messy. His eyes were cloudy, likely coming down from a high. "My name is Jorge," I said, extending my hand.

"I'm Richie," he said, shaking my hand. We greeted each other with the current handshake of the time. He chuckled and sat on a rock next to mine.

"I'm going to get lice from him," I thought, then chastised myself for such a selfish thought. "I'm not here for me," I reminded myself. "Your mom asked me to talk with you," I said.

"Are you from the rehab center?" he asked.

"Do I look like I'm from the rehab center?" I said.

"No," he replied.

I took out a pack of Marlboro Lights and offered him one. He took it, and I lit both our cigarettes. We sat in silence for a while, squinting against the scorching sun.

"Are you from the church?" he asked.

"Do I look like I'm from the church?" I asked.

He looked me over. My old T-shirt had ten holes, and my red-stained sweatpants were rolled up to my knees. My old high-top tennis shoes were held together with duct tape. "No," he said. "You look like you play basketball."

"I do play basketball," I said. "It's my favorite thing to do."

"I played basketball," he said. "I was on the school team."

"I'm on the team," I said. "I made varsity my first year."

"You're tall and skinny. That helps," he said. "Stand up."

I stood up, towering over him by at least six inches.

"Just as I thought. You play center," he said.

"Center? You're crazy," I said. "I'm one of the short ones. You should see the other teams."

"You play in Division One," he said.

"Yes, those guys are monsters," I said.

He chuckled and took a drag of his cigarette. "You shouldn't smoke," he said. "How old are you?"

"I'm sixteen," I said.

His smile widened, revealing missing teeth. "Man, you're tall for sixteen. You play Division One, and you smoke?"

"I drink, too," I said, smiling.

He laughed, spit, and asked, "What are you doing here?"

"I was on my way to visit my friend Rosa when your mom stopped me," I said.

"Where does she live?" he asked.

"She lives down the hill, one of the last houses on the left. She has two cats," I said.

"Oh yes, I know Rosa. She's your friend?"

"Yes, I visit her every week. She's sick," I said.

"I know. My mom told me," he said.

We smoked in silence for a bit. "Why does your mom want me to talk to you?" I asked.

"Because I use drugs," he said.

"Ah, okay," I said.

"You're not going to tell me not to use drugs?" he asked.

"No," I said. "Even though you told me not to smoke," I said, noticing his amusement.

"So why are you here talking to me?" he asked.

"Your mom asked me to," I said.

"So, you were just walking by, and my mom asked you to talk to me?" he asked.

"Yeah, that's what happened," I said.

"You're supposed to help me or something?" he said.

"I don't think so," I said. "Maybe you're supposed to help me. Or maybe I'm supposed to help her?"

He froze for a moment, his eyes vacant. I thought it was the drugs. Then, a tear rolled down his cheek.

"Do you like doing drugs?" I asked.

"I used to," he said. "When I started, it was great. Now I can't stop."

"What are you on?" I asked.

"Whatever I can find. Heroin is too expensive. I use glue, cement, paint thinner, whatever my friends have," he said.

I saw his cigarette was low and handed him the pack. He took one, lit it, and gave the pack back. "Keep it," I said. He smiled—a genuine smile.

"I know my mom is suffering," he said. "I know my cousins and aunts cry and pray for me. I can't leave the drugs," he said, covering his face with his hand. "I don't have any dreams anymore. I want my mom not to suffer," he confided.

"Should I tell him God is love? Does God have a plan for everyone? What should I say?" I thought to myself. I was calm but unsure. "I love my mom," I said.

"I love my mom too," he said.

"Did you tell her?" I asked.

He paused, knowing I knew the answer.

"You should tell her," I said. "I bet you just argue with her when she tells you not to use drugs."

"Yeah," he said. "It's like self-defense, you know?"

"I know," I said.

"How long have you played basketball?" he asked, glancing at my worn, unlaced high-tops.

"I started playing when I was eleven or twelve," I said. "I have two-hour practices every day and practice on weekends."

"That's probably why you're so tall," he said.

"He doesn't know much about genetics," I thought but nodded in agreement.

We talked about basketball, school, girls, and drugs until my friends walked back down the hill.

"I'm out," I said. "These are my homies."

"When will you be back?" he asked.

"Next Saturday," I said. "Can you come look for me?"

"Sure, I'll see you then," I said, shaking his hand.

We all returned to school, and I walked another two miles home. I stored Ricardo and his mother away for the week and returned to my routine.

One week later, I found Ricardo smoking on the same rock.

"What's up, Richie?" I said.

"What's up, George?" he replied, speaking English.

I handed him a Coke. He went inside, returned with a small rum bottle, and poured a shot into his Coke. He gave it to me. "Should I drink this?" I thought. "No, never." I poured a shot into my Coke. "Great, now I'm drinking in the morning," I thought.

I handed him a new pack of Marlboro Lights. He opened it, gave me one, and we continued our conversation like old friends. "I haven't used drugs for a week," he said suddenly.

"He's been waiting to tell me this," I thought. "That's incredible," I said. "How are the withdrawals?"

"Horrible," he said. "It's like torture. I stayed here with my mom, and she helped me."

We talked for hours. Smoking and drinking while we chatted.

"Where is your mom?" I asked.

"She's in church," he said. "She goes every day. She thinks it's a miracle that I'm back."

"What do you think?" I asked.

"It's no miracle," he said. "It's just drugs."

Several hours later, my friends walked by in pairs. "Got to go," I said.

Richie stood up and hugged me. I returned the hug and slapped him hard on the back. "You'll be alright," I said. "Eat something, dude. You're too skinny; chicks don't dig anorexic."

"Stop smoking, kid," he said as I walked away.

"I'll see you next week," I said, waving. He waved back.

I walked back with my friends, feeling proud. I didn't tell anyone about Richie or how he stopped using drugs. I kept the experience to myself, wondering about his mother and his future. Would he get a job? Get married? Maybe go to school and become an English teacher? This is what being a missionary is about—working one-on-one and making a difference. I felt great, better than winning the state basketball championship.

The following week, I went back to Richie's. I whistled outside his door. No movement. I walked closer and called out. His mother came out, hugged me, and sobbed. "Ricardo is dead," she said. "He overdosed yesterday."

I Did Not Invent Marketing Karma...
I Discovered It

Why am I telling you these stories?

The last story teaches us about life, ego, and influence. Even though I wasn't using marketing in the traditional sense, I was still selling and influencing. I wanted Richie to stop using drugs.

Ego played a role in the experience. I wanted to be good at influencing. I needed to be. My motivation wasn't purely altruistic; it was also about satisfying my desire to make a difference, feel important, and win.

What is the lesson from the last story? Ego can drive us to do the right thing, even if our intentions aren't purely charitable. That's how Karma works. It uses your ego, needs, wants, goals, and feelings to motivate you. The question is: How will you use those wants? Use them to generate good Karma. My goals were to help and to be fulfilled. Or, more accurately, to be fulfilled by achieving a specific goal. In this case, assisting Richie in getting off drugs. Your goal could be to change the lives of your employees, your family, or your clients.

When I was sixteen, I wanted to drop out of school and dedicate my life to charity or social work. I held onto this thought for a few years, convinced I could make a difference one person at a time. There was only one catch: I needed my mother's permission. To my surprise, she didn't support my decision. She was a firm believer in finishing college before pursuing anything else. She convinced me I was too young and didn't know what I really wanted. She told me I could change the world after finishing college.

My mother showed me by example that every little action helps, even small gestures like a good example, a smile, honest behavior, and good manners. Little did I know that this one-to-many strategy would become the marketing concept behind the project called "Self Promotion Platform." Using Marketing Karma, online marketing, social networks, and modern advertising tools, these programs help executives and business owners grow their businesses exponentially.

Growing up, I believed I could do anything in life, society, business, charity, or politics. I could be the first Mexican-American president or a professional athlete. Thanks to my Karma, my family, and exposure to underprivileged children and people, I had this belief. I saw people struggling with family, poverty, and drugs. These experiences made me realize how lucky I was to have a wonderful family, education, health, and a home. I was fortunate; half the battle was already won for me. Even in rough times, I reminded myself I was a "lucky bastard."

Lucky Bastard!

So why am I so lucky? I was born in the right place at the right time, just like you. I was born happy, healthy, and wealthy. You might think, "Wait a minute! You grew up without running water, electricity, and a single mom. How is this lucky?" Well, remember, it's all relative.

Yes, I wasn't born in a first-world country, but in Tijuana, next to San Diego, California, I was born very close to it. And I eventually made my way into a first-world country, didn't I? I wasn't born into a wealthy family, but my mother worked hard to send me to the best private school in town. My neighbors didn't have that advantage. I didn't realize I wasn't rich until I was twelve, and I was happy all the same. This has given me an unfair advantage because I always think the worst that could happen financially is being where I was then, with very little money, no electricity, no hot water, and even then, I was incredibly happy. This advantage is almost like cheating!

You are also lucky. I don't know much about you, but I know this: you are fortunate because you can read, and sixteen percent of the world's population can't. You are lucky because you have enough money to buy this book, which probably costs what many people make in a week. If you didn't buy it, you are lucky to have good friends who gave it to you or a library where you can read it. You were born in the rich part of the world's tracks!

You Lucky Bastard!

You are lucky. Remind yourself constantly of why you are so lucky. Do you have a loving spouse, kids, nephews, and parents? Are you healthy? Do you have clothes, food, and shelter? If so, you are luckier than 50 % of the world's population. Think about your good memories, family, and friends. You are all lucky.

Now, the real question is: what will you do with all your luck? It's a good starting place but, indeed, not the goal. What will you do now? If you are not entirely sure, don't worry. I will provide you with a roadmap to help you decide. The decisions you make will surely make you a better person and make others around you better as a consequence. This is one of the powers you will acquire while mastering Marketing Karma and the power of unselfish self-promotion. For starters, use your luck to achieve your dreams. Once you do, once you graduate from being a dreamer, you can step into the real challenge— being a Dream Maker.

Chapter 3
Law 1: The Law of
Cause and Effect

Introduction to
The Law of Cause and Effect

The Law of Cause and Effect is the most well-known law of Karma, often reflected in our lives as what we commonly call "luck." But your actions directly impact your outcomes. Good actions lead to positive results or good karma.

However, we often forget this principle when developing our marketing plans or executing our go-to-market strategies. Creating value for your perfect customer is one of the best ways to harness marketing karma and see immediate rewards.

The Story of How I Discovered the
Great Law of Cause and Effect

As a child and teenager attending a Catholic school, I aspired to be a missionary. I learned to do good without expecting anything in return, not even eternal salvation.

This meant being kind to my family, friends, and strangers alike.

When I was fifteen, I decided to pursue missionary work, initially in my hometown of Tijuana, Mexico, and later with Indigenous populations in the mountains of Chihuahua and southwest Mexico. Unknowingly, I was applying the law of cause and effect. By being good to others, great things happened to me. I thought everyone was lucky, but as I grew older, I realized it wasn't luck—it reflected my actions.

After high school, I chose business school over missionary work to help my family out of poverty. In college, I continued to apply my unselfish principles, making incredible friends and having great experiences. While I could fill another book with my karma stories, I want to focus on the business side for this one.

When I became an entrepreneur at thirty, I used Cause and Effect to provide value to my leads and prospects, resulting in over twenty-five years of loyal customers. I started creating value with content long before the term "content strategy" existed, when there was no YouTube, Google, webinars, or social media.

As a young software executive, I wrote articles and whitepapers and sent them to owners of food manufacturing companies. My perfect customers were

CEOs of meatpacking plants with sales of $50 to $100 million. We developed a direct mail campaign that included letters, articles, and a way for prospects to request our whitepaper on streamlining manufacturing with software. This campaign alone helped me achieve my goals, leading to my promotion to CEO of USA operations at twenty-eight, earning more than I ever dreamed.

The point of this story is Cause and Effect: by creating extreme value, I received money and a new position. While I didn't expect these rewards, I knew helping others would lead to good outcomes.

How To Prioritize
Cause and Effect to Monetize Karma

Running a business involves many tasks, but the most profitable activity is creating extreme value for prospects. During COVID-19, we survived by providing value when traditional methods like trade shows were unavailable. We wrote a whitepaper on the Hemp Industry and promoted it with videos on various social media platforms. This whitepaper and a simple funnel saved our business by attracting hemp entrepreneurs.

The Great Law of Cause and Effect is foundational for all other laws of Karma in this book. To apply it in your business, consider the most significant value you can provide your perfect customer and develop a strategy to deliver it. Follow up using email, text, calls, or social media.

Multiply Yourself Using Cause and Effect

Now that you understand Cause and Effect, it's time to automate your marketing and sales to attract prospects in large numbers. One effective method is the one-to-many marketing campaign, where you sell to many people simultaneously.

A one-to-many campaign could include podcasts, social media videos, or live seminars. My favorite is webinars, especially evergreen webinars that deliver massive value and can be automated.

As a young software executive and later as an entrepreneur, I perfected the one-to-many strategy, using it to sell various products and services.

Examples and Exercises for Cause and Effect

Summary: Whatever you put out into the universe comes back to you. Ethical marketing and genuine customer engagement will lead to loyal clients and a positive brand reputation. Create massive value, get enormous value!

Understanding the Concept

The Great Law emphasizes that every action has a corresponding reaction. In marketing, this means your business conduct and customer interactions will directly impact your success. Ethical behavior, honesty, and quality lead to positive outcomes.

Applying the Law to Your Business

1. **Ethical Marketing**
   - o **Transparency:** Ensure all marketing materials accurately represent your products or services.
   - o **Honesty:** Be upfront about any potential downsides or limitations.
2. **Genuine Customer Engagement**
   - o **Personalized Interactions:** Understand your customers' needs and provide a tailored experience.
   - o **Responsive Communication:** Address inquiries and complaints promptly and professionally.
3. **Value-Driven Marketing**
   - o **Content Marketing:** Create and share valuable content that addresses your customers' pain points and interests.
   - o **Community Involvement:** Participate in local events and support charitable causes.

Examples of Small Business Owners

1. **The Ethical Coffee Shop:** Sarah sources fair-trade coffee beans and uses environmentally friendly

packaging. Her transparency and community engagement have made her coffee shop a beloved community spot.
2. **The Honest Handyman:** Mike provides honest and reliable service, sharing DIY tips and avoiding unnecessary upselling. His integrity has earned him a loyal customer base and positive reviews.

Key Takeaways

- Ethical behavior pays off.
- Engagement matters.
- Value creation enhances brand reputation.
- One-to-many marketing saves time and effort.

Exercises

1. **Evaluate Your Marketing Materials:** Ensure transparency and honesty in all your marketing.
2. **Customer Feedback Loop:** Collect and analyze customer feedback to make improvements.
3. **Content Plan:** Develop a content marketing plan that provides value to your customers.
4. **Community Engagement:** Identify opportunities for local involvement and track the impact.

Conclusion

The Great Law of Cause and Effect is a powerful reminder that ethical behavior and genuine customer engagement are crucial for business success. Embrace the principles of Marketing Karma to build a loyal customer base and a positive brand reputation. Your actions today will shape the future of your business.

The Great Law of Cause and Effect

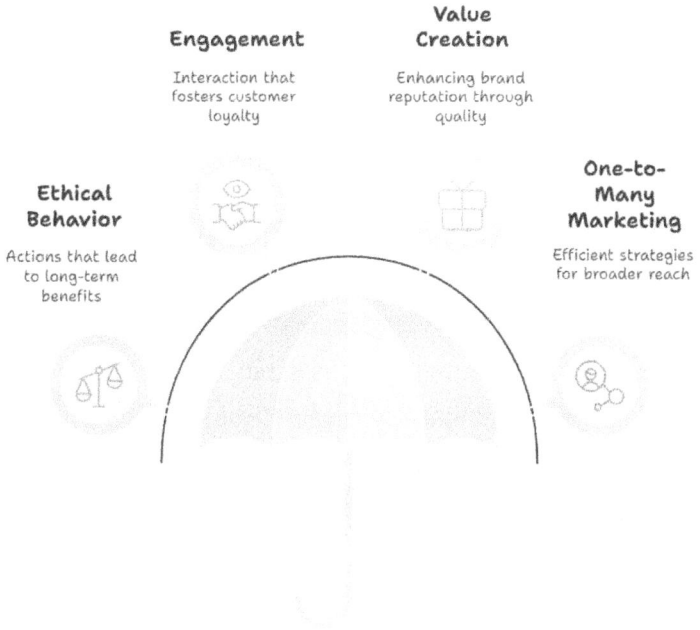

Engagement

Interaction that
fosters customer
loyalty

**Value
Creation**

Enhancing brand
reputation through
quality

**Ethical
Behavior**

Actions that lead
to long-term
benefits

**One-to-
Many
Marketing**

Efficient strategies
for broader reach

Figure 5 - The Great Law of Cause and Effect

Chapter 4
Law 2: The Law of Creation

Introduction to The Law of Creation

Creating products, services, content, and value is vital to Karma. As discussed in The Great Law, creating content, webinars, and value is a significant part of marketing karma. In this law, you can use your creativity to produce books, whitepapers, articles, videos, and other forms of value for your perfect consumer.

As you may have noticed, I love writing. It's one of my favorite ways to contribute to society. I write business books, motivational ones, and even science fiction and fantasy. Despite running a business, I've found a way to grow it by creating books, webinars, videos, and courses.

Become a Creator of Happiness

Creators are not limited to video creators or social media influencers; they include artists and anyone who engages in creative endeavors. You are a creator because you can create art, and if it doesn't come easy to you right now, it's only because you haven't been using your creativity as much as you should. Please take this opportunity to embrace your creative nature, use it for yourself, and provide value to others. This value will return to you, often in more significant measure than what you put in.

I created my first book, "Build Your Beverage Empire," to help entrepreneurs start their beverage businesses. There were no books or information on the subject; it seemed like a big secret. I knew it would bring some karma, but I never imagined it would lead to sending five companies public, creating hundreds of beverages, and traveling the world. I didn't create any funnels or content; people just called me out of the blue to tell me, "I read your book; it changed my life, and I need to hire you." That's karma!

Creation extends beyond content to products. I've worked with Snoop Dogg and other musicians, NFL and NBA players, and actors to develop and manufacture beverages, vitamins, hemp and mushroom products, and other consumer packaged goods. I've helped thousands of entrepreneurs create and sell their products. As a creative director, I imagine products and bring them to life with packaging, art, branding, and manufacturing. When you create solutions, think of the benefits to your customers first—solve their problems, make them happy, and be a creator of happiness!

Examples and Exercises
for The Law of Creation

Law of Creation Summary

Life doesn't just happen; it requires our participation.

Marketing Karma Adaptation

Your business's success requires proactive marketing and engagement. Create opportunities and content that reflect your values and attract like-minded customers.

Introduction

The Law of Creation highlights the necessity of proactive engagement and active participation in shaping our reality. For small business owners, this means taking deliberate steps to create opportunities, generate valuable content, and engage meaningfully with your audience. By actively participating in your business's growth and development, you can ensure that your marketing efforts align with your values and attract customers who resonate with your mission.

Understanding the Concept

The Law of Creation is based on the idea that we are co-creators of our reality. In marketing, this means your success is not a matter of chance but the result of proactive efforts. You can influence your business's trajectory by creating valuable content, engaging with your audience, and fostering a positive brand image.

Applying the Law to Your Business

1. **Proactive Marketing:**
   o **Strategic Planning:** Develop a comprehensive marketing plan that outlines your goals, target audience, and critical strategies. For example, if you own a yoga studio, your plan might include social media campaigns, email newsletters, and partnerships with local wellness influencers.
   o **Consistent Execution:** Regularly execute your marketing strategies to maintain momentum. Consistency builds brand recognition and customer trust. A local bakery could post daily updates on fresh bakes, customer testimonials, and special promotions.
2. **Value Creation:**
   o **Content Marketing:** Create and share content that provides value to your audience. This could include blog posts, videos, podcasts, or social media updates. For example, a gardening business could create instructional videos on seasonal planting tips.
   o **Educational Resources:** Offer free resources that educate and inform your customers. This builds trust and positions you as an expert. A financial advisor could

provide downloadable guides on budgeting and saving for retirement.

3. **Engagement:**
   - **Customer Interaction:** Actively engage with your customers through various channels. Respond to comments, answer questions, and encourage feedback. A small café could engage with customers on Instagram by sharing behind-the-scenes content and responding to customer stories.
   - **Community Building:** Foster a sense of community around your brand. This could involve hosting events, creating online forums, or participating in local initiatives. A boutique fitness studio might host free outdoor workout sessions or wellness workshops.

Examples of Small Business Owners

1. **The Active Florist:** Emily owns a small florist shop. She regularly creates content for her blog and social media channels, including flower arrangement tutorials, care tips, and behind-the-scenes looks at her shop. She engages with her followers by responding to comments and sharing user-generated content. Emily also participates in local farmers' markets and collaborates with other small businesses for events. Her proactive approach has built a loyal customer base and positioned her as a go-to expert in her community.

2. **The Strategic Accountant:** John is a freelance accountant helping small businesses. He regularly publishes articles and videos on financial management, tax preparation, and business

planning. John also offers free webinars and workshops to educate small business owners on financial literacy. By providing valuable content and engaging with his audience, John has established himself as a trusted advisor, leading to a steady stream of referrals and new clients.

Key Takeaways

- Proactivity is Essential: Success in marketing and business requires active participation and consistent effort.
- Create Value: Providing valuable content and resources builds trust and positions you as an expert.
- Engage with Your Audience: Active engagement fosters loyalty and strengthens your **brand community.**

Exercises

1. **Develop a Marketing Plan:**
   o Outline your marketing goals, target audience, and critical strategies. Identify the platforms and channels where you will focus your efforts.
   o Create a content calendar to ensure consistent execution. Plan your posts, campaigns, and events ahead of time.
2. **Content Creation:**
   o Identify topics that would be valuable to your audience. Consider their needs, interests, and challenges.
   o Create various content types, including blog posts, videos, infographics, and podcasts.

Aim to provide actionable insights and helpful information.

3. **Customer Engagement:**
   - Choose one social media platform to focus on and commit to engaging with your audience daily. Respond to comments, share user-generated content, and initiate conversations.
   - Plan a community-building activity, such as a live Q&A session, a webinar, or a local event. Use this opportunity to connect with your audience on a personal level.

Conclusion

The Law of Creation emphasizes the importance of proactive engagement and value creation in achieving business success. You can build a robust and ethical brand that attracts loyal customers by actively participating in your marketing efforts, creating valuable content, and engaging with your audience. Remember, your business's success is not a matter of chance but of deliberate actions and consistent efforts. Embrace the principles of Marketing Karma and take an active role in shaping your business's future.

The Law of Creation

Audience Engagement

Fostering loyalty strengthens brand community

Value Creation

Offering valuable content builds trust

Proactive Engagement

Active participation drives business success

Figure 6 - The Law of Creation

Chapter 5
Big Picture Promotion

Personal Branding for Life

"Don't promote for today. Don't promote for tomorrow. Promote for life."

Big Picture Promotion applies to your life and your business; it's your personal brand in front of your family and friends and your business audience composed of your customers, employees, suppliers, investors, and board of directors.

In your personal brand, pay close attention to developing a well-structured brand that includes your personality, oral and written communication, clothing, and personal appearance, including your hair, skin, and even your weight. If you're well-shaven and dressed, your skin is crackling because you don't use a moisturizer, or your hair is dirty or snowing dandruff, your audience will focus on these details.

"Come back here and iron that shirt," my grandmother would say.

"I'm running late," I would answer.

"It's better to be late and look good," she would say.

This was an ongoing battle when I was eight to ten years old.

"Tuck in that shirt, shine your shoes, put on a belt," my grandmother told me. This stuck with me at a basic level.

"You don't have to be rich to look good and clean," she would often say. My grandmother made her own clothes; she always looked fancy, with silk scarves, tailored suits, work outfits, and beautiful radiating skin.

Think of your promotions as a lifelong effort that transcends your knowledge and experience in a particular subject or your position as an authority in an industry. Think big picture. Think of promotions for life. My mother and aunts dressed the same way. I often wear scars or bandanas around my neck in remembrance of my grandmother.

Consider a long-term strategy when branding a company, a product, or yourself. When running a digital marketing campaign, don't just run ads to see what happens; instead, test every aspect of your advertising, including your headline, buttons, images, videos, audience, and copy. I test these individually with twenty to fifty different assets per campaign. This might sound like brain damage, but it's not, and the results are up to ten times as good as if you just run an ad with split testing.

Your Big Picture Promotion is your life plan. It is your positioning statement for the next twenty to fifty years. It positions you in business, the community, and politics—not just today or tomorrow but forever. This strategy doesn't have a specific call to action. It doesn't prompt you to get a job, land a business deal, or even launch a nonprofit organization. This is even bigger than that. This strategy goes beyond business, the community, and politics. It is your promotional spirit. It promotes your character, your principles, and yourself.

Why Do You Need to Think Big Picture?

How will I benefit from Big Picture Promotions? What are the practical applications?

These are essential questions. Throughout life, you and many others will make decisions that affect others. You will make recommendations and judgments, build teams, and work with others. When all these decisions are made, when you have to work with someone, hire someone, promote someone in their job, look for a partner, a political candidate, or just someone of value, who will you choose? This decision is not just for you to make; everyone makes these decisions throughout life. This is where the practical application of Big Picture Promotions comes in. When you apply your Marketing Karma strategies long-term, your phone will be ringing—not just for a job or a promotion, but for everything. This won't happen once; you will start seeing more and more people getting close to you, being attracted to you. It's like supercharging your promotional magnets.

Without Big Picture Promotions, your new promotion is just short-term. You may get a good response for a month or two, a year or two, or for a product or a business. But eventually, it will vanish, and you will have to start all over again. Therefore, you need your Big Picture Promotion. You need to always stay on top of the promotional stack. You must always be the first person others call for any project or party.

Yes, you will learn other specific applications for promotions. You will learn how to apply them to get a job, a promotion, or a higher salary. You will learn how to sell products and services and how to fund a business or grow it. There are many specific applications for your promotions. If you are currently looking for a better job, running for political office, opening a business, or need a promotion for your project, it's hard to think big picture. It isn't easy because you have a necessity now. You need to sell now. You are driven. You need to promote your business. You are fast and furious! Yes, all of this is great.

And, like we said, you can promote very specifically and successfully. But you will have other projects, businesses, and situations, so think big picture and think for life when you can.

"Promote for life, not for a job, a project, or a business."

My Fifteen-Year Mentoring Funnel

How long should your marketing campaigns last? It's up to you, but I want to work on a meaningful campaign, take my time, and make it last forever. This is what I did when I started consulting for Consumer Goods companies, primarily vitamin and beverage companies.

After I sold my first wholesale distribution company, I had a good online following, with over thirty thousand email subscribers. I decided to sell consulting to my followers, but then I switched to coaching and, finally, to mentoring. If you're wondering what the difference is, it's pretty significant. Let me explain.

A consultant does the work for the client, a coach is generic, you don't need to specialize, and the mentor is the guru, specializing in a particular industry, in this case, wholesale distribution, beverages, and nutraceuticals. As a coach, I gave keynote speeches and was a marketing mastermind; I was even Dan Kennedy's CMO at his direct response company, the most famous copywriter still alive. As a mentor, I help CEOs and founders succeed in specific industries or sectors.

I built a funnel more than fifteen years ago to capture leads and sell mentoring, and I haven't changed much over the years. Sure, I added new technology, such as better CRMs and autoresponders, social media campaigns, and lately, Artificial Intelligence, but the primary funnel is the same: a squeeze page to capture emails and phone numbers, sharing knowledge for free, selling books and courses, and finally, selling mentoring, mastermind groups, and other services.

You don't need to be a consultant, coach, or mentor to apply these strategies; they apply to writers and service providers that I call artisans (accountants, lawyers, doctors, etc.) or even those selling consumer goods.

The idea is to build one fantastic campaign, not ten mediocre ones!

Key Takeaways

1. **Think Long-Term**: Your promotions should be a lifelong effort, not just for immediate needs.
2. **Consistent Behavior**: Your actions should consistently reflect your character and principles.
3. **Big Picture Mindset**: Adopt a broader perspective in all your promotional activities.
4. **Sustainable Impact**: Aim to create a lasting impression that endures beyond specific projects or goals.

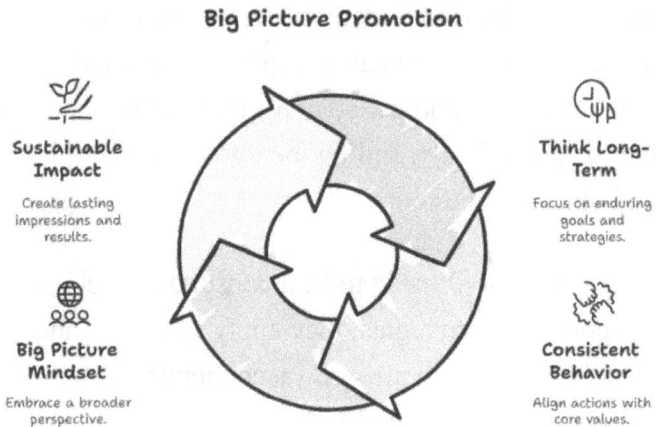

Big Picture Promotion

Sustainable Impact

Create lasting impressions and results.

Think Long-Term

Focus on enduring goals and strategies.

Big Picture Mindset

Embrace a broader perspective.

Consistent Behavior

Align actions with core values.

Figure 7 - Big Picture Promotion

Practical Steps

1. **Define Your Core Values**: Know what you stand for and let it guide your promotions.

2. **Invest in Relationships**: Build and nurture connections that will support you long-term.
3. **Be Authentic**: Ensure your promotions reflect your true self, not just a façade.
4. **Adapt and Evolve**: Stay relevant by continuously learning and adapting your strategies.

By embracing Big Picture Promotion, you set the stage for sustained success and lasting influence. This approach ensures that your promotional efforts are not just for immediate gains but contribute to a legacy of integrity and impact.

Examples of Big Picture Promotion

1. Building a Personal Brand

Example: Oprah Winfrey

Strategy: Oprah built her personal brand by consistently showcasing authenticity, empathy, and a commitment to empowering others. From her early days on "The Oprah Winfrey Show" to her publishing, film, and philanthropy ventures, she has maintained a consistent message of personal growth and social impact.

Big Picture Impact: Oprah's brand is synonymous with trust and inspiration. Her long-term commitment to these values has made her a beloved figure worldwide, allowing her to influence millions and create a lasting legacy.

Takeaway: Focus on your core values and ensure they are reflected in every aspect of your professional and personal life.

2. Establishing Thought Leadership

Example: Simon Sinek

Strategy: Simon Sinek established himself as a thought leader through his book "Start With Why" and his influential TED Talk. He consistently shares insights on leadership, motivation, and organizational culture, positioning himself as an expert in these fields.

Big Picture Impact: Sinek's long-term commitment to understanding and teaching leadership principles has made him a go-to authority. His ideas have influenced business leaders, educators, and entrepreneurs globally.

Takeaway: Continuously share your knowledge and insights to build a reputation as a thought leader in your field.

3. Creating a Legacy Through Innovation

Example: Steve Jobs

Strategy: Steve Jobs focused on creating innovative products that changed industries. His vision for Apple was not just about technology but about creating products that enhanced people's lives. Jobs' emphasis on design, user experience, and innovation has impacted the tech industry.

Big Picture Impact: Jobs' approach ensured that Apple became a brand associated with innovation and quality. His legacy continues to influence the company and the tech industry long after his passing.

Takeaway: Focus on innovation and long-term impact, not just short-term gains.

4. Philanthropy and Social Impact

Example: Bill and Melinda Gates

Strategy: After achieving massive success with Microsoft, Bill and Melinda Gates turned their attention to philanthropy. Through the Bill & Melinda Gates Foundation, they address global issues such as health care, education, and poverty.

Big Picture Impact: Their long-term commitment to social causes has significantly impacted global health and development. Their work continues to influence philanthropic efforts worldwide.

Takeaway: Use your resources and influence to impact society, creating a lasting legacy positively.

5. Consistent Ethical Behavior

Example: Warren Buffett

Strategy: Warren Buffett, known as the "Oracle of Omaha," has built his reputation through consistent ethical behavior and long-term investment strategies. He emphasizes integrity, transparency, and patience in his investment philosophy.

Big Picture Impact: Buffett's ethical approach to business has earned him immense respect and trust. His reputation has made Berkshire Hathaway a highly regarded company in the investment community.

Takeaway: Maintain high ethical standards and consistency in your professional dealings to build lasting trust and respect.

Implementing Big Picture Promotion

1. **Define Your Vision**: Establish a clear, long-term vision for your career and personal brand. What do you want to be known for in 20, 30, or 50 years?
2. **Align Your Actions**: Ensure your daily actions and decisions align with your long-term vision and values.
3. **Invest in Relationships**: Build and nurture meaningful relationships that support and enhance your journey.

4. **Adapt and Evolve**: Stay open to learning and evolving. The world and your strategies change, but your core values should remain constant.
5. **Focus on Impact**: Think about the broader impact of your work and how it contributes to society. Aim for sustainable, positive change.

By thinking big picture and promoting for life, you ensure that your efforts create a lasting, meaningful legacy. This approach benefits you and contributes to the well-being and success of those around you.

Maintaining Long-Term Promotions

Maintaining long-term promotions requires consistent effort, strategic thinking, and a focus on building and nurturing relationships. Here are some key strategies to help you sustain long-term promotion:

1. Consistency is Key

Example: Coca-Cola

Strategy: Coca-Cola has maintained a consistent brand message for over a century. Their marketing focuses on happiness, sharing, and timeless moments.

Implementation:

- Ensure that your core message and values remain consistent across all platforms and over time.

- Regularly update your content to reflect current trends while staying true to your brand identity.

2. Build and Nurture Relationships

Example: Networking Events

Strategy: Attend industry conferences, seminars, and workshops to build relationships with peers, potential clients, and influencers both online and offline.

Implementation:

- Follow up with contacts you meet at events to maintain and deepen these relationships.
- Follow your new contacts on LinkedIn first; then, on Twitter, you can use TikTok, Instagram, and others.
- Offer value to your network through knowledge sharing, support, and collaboration. I like sending articles, whitepapers, and videos to help my contacts reach their pains and goals.

3. Continuous Learning and Adaptation

Example: Google

Strategy: Google continually evolves its products and services based on user feedback and technological advancements.

Implementation:

- Stay updated with industry trends and advancements. Be a guru in your industry!
- Invest in personal and professional development through courses, reading, and attending relevant events.

4. Engage Your Audience

Example: Social Media Interaction

Strategy: Engage with your audience regularly through social media, blogs, and newsletters.

Implementation:

- Respond to comments, messages, and feedback promptly.
- Create interactive content such as polls, Q&A sessions, and live videos to engage your audience.
- Start a LinkedIn newsletter; for example, I have newsletters on marketing, leadership, funding, beverages, and the hemp/cannabis industry.

5. Provide Value

Example: Educational Content

Strategy: Share valuable content that educates, informs, and helps your audience.

Implementation:

- Write blog posts, articles, and whitepapers that address common challenges and provide solutions.
- Host webinars and workshops to share your expertise and provide practical insights.
- Write books, yes, books! It takes a bit to write them, but it organizes your ideas and provides truckloads of value to your contacts.

6. Leverage Public Relations

Example: Press Releases and Media Coverage

Strategy: Use public relations to maintain a positive image and increase visibility.

Implementation:

- Develop strong relationships with journalists and media outlets.
- Regularly send press releases about significant achievements, new products, or critical company news.
- Use HARO or Help a Reporter Out, a free service that sends daily queries from reporters. I've gotten on the NYT, Wall Street Journal, Forbes, Success, and hundreds more.

7. Monitor and Measure Your Efforts

Example: Analytics Tools

Strategy: Use analytics tools to track the effectiveness of your promotional strategies.

Implementation:

- Monitor key metrics such as engagement, reach, and conversion rates.
- Adjust your strategies based on data insights to improve your long-term promotion efforts.
- You can find your buyer persona or avatar using free online analytic tools: Probe Google, Meta, TikTok, LinkedIn, and your website traffic or social media followers.

8. Authenticity and Transparency

Example: Patagonia

Strategy: Patagonia is known for its commitment to environmental sustainability and transparency in its business practices.

Implementation:

- Be honest and transparent in your communications and actions.
- Share your successes and challenges and how you're working to overcome them.
- Share stories, not pitches, and be vulnerable; tell the viewer or reader what you did wrong, and take responsibility and let the reader cheer for you!

9. Create a Strong Online Presence

Example: Personal Website and Blog

Strategy: Develop a comprehensive online presence through a personal website, blog, and active social media profiles.

Implementation:

- Regularly update your website and blog with fresh content.
- Maintain active and engaging profiles on relevant social media platforms.
- Send emails at least once per week. If you can't change your business model to do this, it will change your life.

10. Seek and Act on Feedback

Example: Customer Surveys

Strategy: Regularly seek feedback from your audience, clients, and peers.

Implementation:

- Conduct surveys and polls to gather insights on your performance.
- Act on the feedback to improve your products, services, and overall approach.

11. Stay True to Your Values

Example: Ethical Business Practices

Strategy: Always adhere to your core values and principles, even when faced with challenges.

Implementation:

- Make decisions that align with your values and ethical standards.
- Communicate your values clearly and consistently to your audience.

Integrating these strategies into your long-term promotional efforts allows you to build and maintain a strong, lasting presence that supports your professional and personal growth. Remember, long-term promotion is not a one-time effort but a continuous process that requires dedication and adaptability.

Your Personal Brand
Across Projects and Companies

Your personality is also part of your brand, products, services, and company. I've launched over one thousand Fast Moving Consumer Goods, including vitamins, beverages, gummies, tools, clothing, pet supplies, car accessories, electronics, and much more. I've branded products for Snoop Dogg, Rick Ross, Dennis Rodman, Cheech and Chong, and my own companies and brands, even taking a few of them public in the USA. I've also raised and helped raise over one hundred million dollars in funding, exported products to Mexico, and more. Across these projects, I've always sold myself instead of my company or logo, using my personal brand to leverage my audience.

Your personality is also part of your brand. This includes what you show inside and outside, such as your expressions, knowledge, speech patterns, and knowledge. One secret weapon is your smile. It can close the deal and create trust, make people feel welcome, and show you're a nice person all at once. Try it as an experiment; smile at everyone for a week, in the supermarket, at work, even walking down the street. The results might astonish you!

Chapter 6
You Are Not Your Job

What Do You Want to Be
When You Grow Up?

One of the "Promotion Traps" we fall into is defining ourselves by our current job or occupation. We might see ourselves as a salesperson, an executive, a lawyer, a musician, or a soccer mom. The truth is that we are much more complex. We can be multiple things at different times, even simultaneously.

Picture yourself at a cocktail party, engaged in conversations. Inevitably, someone will ask, "What do you do?" This question often means, "Where do you work?" or "What type of business are you in?" Your answer could pigeonhole you in their minds. You don't want to be remembered merely as "Bob, the insurance guy" or "Mike, the lawyer." You are more than your job title. You could be an investor, a philosopher, or a dancer—all at once.

So, what do you say when people ask about your job? This is the perfect time to practice your promotion and leave a lasting impression. Be careful not to limit yourself by your occupation or hobby. Instead, tell them who you are. Be specific and say you're a lover, a visionary, or a poet. Don't just say you're a warehouse manager; that's not who you are.

This is where your newfound Marketing Karma knowledge comes into play. Start listening instead of talking. When asked about what you do, turn the question back on them. Show genuine interest in others. I'm rarely asked first what I do because I'm always sincerely interested in others. I ask pressing questions to learn about them. When I have valuable advice, a book recommendation, or a story that could help them, then I share it. After offering sincere help, they often turn to me and ask, "What do you do?" That's when I can mention my work in marketing, writing, mentoring, entrepreneurship, or other areas.

This approach isn't limited to business or cocktail parties. It applies to everyday situations—buying a car, dealing with family issues, etc. Remember, you are not just promoting your business skills; you are promoting yourself.

Even in important meetings at the office, someone might introduce me as CMO, and when I talk about finances, production, or funding, our visitors ask me, "I thought you were the CMO." Yes, being the CMO is great; I love it. However, I'm also a co-founder of a portfolio of companies, and I play different roles in product development and capital raising. How can you introduce yourself at a social gathering or a business meeting? You can work on witty, funny ways to be remembered.

Jumping Ship

I receive many sales calls related to my various businesses. Salespeople pitch everything from food and insurance to gas, supplies, and cars. Over the years, I've become acquainted with some who try to sell me business-related products and services. I've been in the beverage industry for a while, and many people seek my advice or propose business opportunities.

These salespeople often jump ship to another company or product, calling me with the same pitch for something new. They always claim the new product is the best. I tell them, "I bet on the jockey, not the horse." It's not just the product that matters but the people behind it—the manager, owner, or entrepreneur. Sell yourself first, not just your product or business. You may have different products, businesses, goals, and passions, but promote yourself above all.

Promote yourself, not your job, hobby, or business. You have much more to offer than your occupation.

What Will You Be When You Grow Up?

Hopefully, you remain a kid at heart. As children, we imagine being different things at different times—

Superman, a firefighter, a princess. We tell kids they can be anything they want if they put their minds to it. What about us, the kids at heart? What will we be when we grow up? Personally, I don't know yet. Why would I want to grow up? Let's teach our children and ourselves to be everything.

Think of your dreams, hobbies, and aspirations. Our thoughts and dreams evolve, and that's perfectly fine. We need to experience, learn, and move to the next dream. Be an entrepreneur, a poet, a painter, a dancer, or a teacher. Why not? Ask yourself what you dream of being—everything and anything!

Start by making a crazy list of what you want to do when you grow up. Please write it down without categorizing it by age. Focus on experiences rather than material possessions.

Chapter 7
Teaching Your Child to Laugh

ABS – Always Be Smiling

Your smile is a promotional tool you use everywhere, every day, all the time. It's a permanent part of your promotional toolbox. You can't shake it or take it off, and it's always there. The beauty of a smile is that it's not just for show, not just for promotion. Smiling and laughing promote you from the inside. They help you be happy and healthy. Wearing a smile should be part of you, your image, personality, and character. It reflects how you see yourself, your life, the world, and the situations around you. Laughter is a magnet. It attracts people to you, making them wonder why you're happy, what you know, and what you're smiling about. There's a particular mystery about a person who is always smiling.

Laughter is a natural, instinctive impulse, but it can also be taught. Imagine making it a point to teach every child to smile—your kids, grandkids, nephews, nieces, all kids. It's important to teach children to laugh, starting as babies, and encouraging them to laugh loudly and often. As they grow older, please continue to make it a point to laugh with them and show them how to keep laughing, even in times of sorrow.

Big Surprise – It's Not All Laughs

I was surprised to learn that not everyone smiles all the time. People started asking me a few years back why I was always smiling. Others noticed that every family member was always smiling, even laughing out loud in times of happiness and trying to do so in times of sorrow. These comments surprised me. I thought laughing and smiling were normal for every family until I sadly discovered they weren't. I decided to write about it.

In my family, adults and even kids teach babies to smile. We're constantly making them laugh; I never thought anything of it. I assumed this happened all over the world in every single family. I see now that it doesn't, but it must. Smiling is one of the most magnetic tools you have in your toolbox. It attracts people to you, makes them wonder why you're happy or if you're always excited, and makes people feel good and at ease.

I've always tried to have a smile on my face. I'm happy most of the time, smiling all the time. People comment on it, especially friends and family. My wife finds it amusing that I always wake up with a big smile on my face. She likes it and now tries to do the same. It's a powerful motivational and self-help strategy, and I never thought it was such a powerful promotional tool.

Trade Show Smile

I attend many trade shows throughout the year, but one stands out. I represented one of my businesses and sold products to supermarkets. I remember approaching people passing by, starting conversations, answering their questions, and offering samples and brochures of our products. It was no different from other trade shows I'd attended. Some booth visitors noticed my smile and asked if I was happy. I told them I was. They said, "You look happy, energetic, and always smiling." I thought nothing of it; it wasn't the first time people asked if I was happy.

Later, someone else asked, "Why are you smiling?" I answered, "Because I'm happy." They laughed and continued on their way. Later, these people returned with a colleague, a buyer at a large, well-known company. They told him, "Here's the happy guy I told you about." They didn't mention my company or products, only that I was the happy guy. In the back of my mind, I made a mental note. I realized people do notice. I wondered if people were telling me about it and how many were thinking about it. I started being conscientious about smiling and observed people's comments and reactions.

I was surprised when person after person commented on why I was always smiling—in meetings, at social gatherings, and even in long, cold boardroom meetings. I also noticed that not everyone smiled, not even a little bit. This was a big shocker to me. I asked myself, "Why aren't they smiling? Are they unhappy, or do they not want to show they're happy?" The more I saw people not smiling, the more I thought they were in pain, stressed, or depressed. Why don't they smile? Aren't they Happy, Healthy, and Wealthy? Remember, ABS—Always Be Smiling!

Smiling at the Doctor

I decided to add "Smiling & Laughter" to your promotional toolbox after a doctor's visit. I'd talked about smiling before; I even wrote a short story about it called "Teaching Your Child to Laugh," like the title of this chapter. Although it had been in my mind as something you need to do to be happy, I never imagined I'd include it in this promotional book until that doctor's appointment earlier this year.

I went to the doctor for a checkup. I was in a lot of back pain and needed to get it checked out. My wife decided to go with me and drive me there, and as we were leaving, my mother arrived for a visit. I told her where we were headed, and she decided to tag along. (No, I don't usually take my mom to my doctor's appointments; it was a coincidence.) Once there, the nurse came to the waiting room and called my name. I stood up with a big smile on my face. She took my blood pressure and other vitals before sending me to see the doctor. As I was leaving, I stopped at her nurse station to thank her with a smile, and she told me, "You came in with a smile, and now you're leaving with a smile. We don't see many people smiling when they come to the doctor. Thank you for smiling! Your mother did a great job teaching you to smile. Tell her for me the next time you see her."

I did not know this nurse. I had never seen her, but she made a point. So, I said to her, "You can tell her yourself; she's outside in the waiting room." And she did. The nurse came out to the waiting room and thanked my mother. Wow, I needed to write and share this with others. Never underestimate the power of a smile. It will always positively affect you and others.

Smile to Yourself!

Smiling and laughing are more than just emotional responses. They have physiological benefits that can positively impact your overall well-being. Research shows that smiling releases endorphins, serotonin, and dopamine—neurotransmitters that improve mood and reduce stress. This biological reaction reinforces the habit of smiling, creating a positive feedback loop that enhances your health and happiness.

"Smile When You're Alone, It Will Make You Happy."

When you teach children to smile and laugh, you're encouraging a positive attitude and promoting their physical health. Laughter boosts the immune system, lowers blood pressure, and improves heart health. By fostering a habit of smiling and laughing in your children, you set them up for a lifetime of health benefits.

Cultivating a Habit of Happiness

Teaching children to smile starts with leading by example. They will mimic your behavior if they see you smiling and laughing often. Make it a point to create joyful moments with your family—tell jokes, play games, and engage in fun activities that elicit laughter.

Encourage your children to find humor in everyday situations. Help them see the lighter side of life, even when faced with challenges. This perspective makes life more enjoyable and builds resilience, teaching them to cope with stress and adversity more effectively.

Practical Tips for Always Be Smiling (ABS)

1. **Start the Day with a Smile**: Make a conscious effort to smile as soon as you wake up. It sets a positive tone for the rest of the day.

2. **Practice Gratitude**: Regularly reflect on the things you're grateful for. Gratitude fosters a positive mindset, making it easier to smile and laugh.
3. **Surround Yourself with Positive Influences**: Spend time with people who uplift and inspire you. Their positivity will rub off on you, making it easier to maintain a habit of smiling.
4. **Find Humor in Everyday Life**: Look for the funny side of situations. This doesn't mean ignoring serious issues but finding balance by appreciating humor where it naturally occurs.
5. **Engage in Activities That Make You Happy**: Pursue hobbies and interests that bring you joy. The more you engage in activities you love, the more naturally you'll smile.
6. **Smile at Strangers**: A simple smile can brighten someone's day. Make it a habit to smile at people you meet, from the barista at your coffee shop to colleagues at work.

Pathways to a Brighter Smile

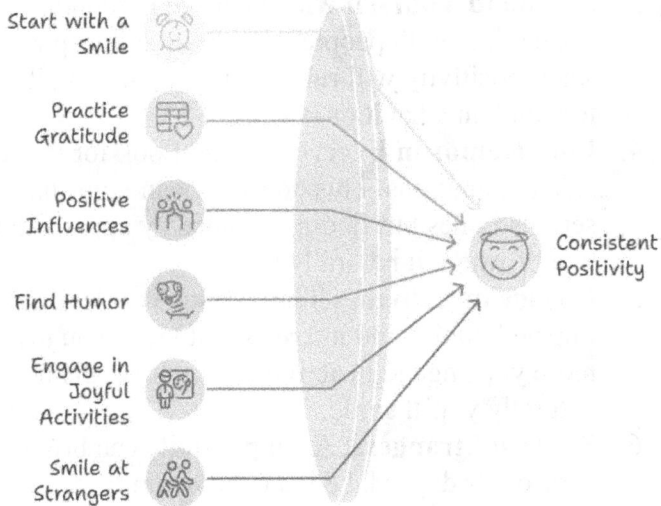

Start with a Smile

Practice Gratitude

Positive Influences

Find Humor

Engage in Joyful Activities

Smile at Strangers

Consistent Positivity

Figure 8 - Pathways to a Brighter Smile

Teaching Your Child to Laugh: A Lifelong Gift

When you teach your child to laugh, you give them a lifelong gift. Laughter builds social bonds, improves mental health, and fosters a positive outlook on life. Here are some strategies to help you teach your child to laugh:

1. **Be Playful**: Engage in silly activities, make funny faces, and tell jokes. Your playful attitude will encourage your child to laugh.

2. **Create a Joyful Environment**: Fill your home with laughter by playing fun music, watching comedies, and encouraging spontaneous dance parties.
3. **Share Funny Stories**: Tell your child humorous stories from your life or read them funny books. Sharing laughter strengthens your bond and promotes a positive atmosphere.
4. **Encourage Social Interaction**: Arrange playdates with other children who have a good sense of humor. Social interactions with peers can enhance your child's ability to find joy in shared experiences.
5. **Model Resilience**: Show your child how to find humor in setbacks. Laughing at minor mishaps teaches them to approach life resiliently and optimistically.

A Smile That Resonates

Your smile is a powerful tool that resonates with people. It's not just a fleeting expression; it's a reflection of your inner state and a magnet that attracts others to you. When you make smiling a habit, you create a positive environment around you, making people feel comfortable and valued.

In the business world, a genuine smile can be your secret weapon. It sets you apart, makes you memorable, and creates a lasting impression. People are more likely to do business with someone who exudes positivity and warmth. Your smile can open doors, build relationships, and enhance your professional reputation.

Smiling Through Challenges

After a terrible accident that left me bedridden for years, in horrible around-the-clock pain, and with several Traumatic Brain Injuries, I had to put my positivity to the test, and with a smile on my face, I'm still battling to recover. My body language is part of my recovery; it all starts with a smile!

Life is complex, and maintaining a smile during tough times can be challenging. However, it's during these times that a smile can be most potent. Smiling in the face of adversity shows strength and resilience. It can uplift your spirits and those around you.

Remember, smiling doesn't mean ignoring your problems. It means choosing to face them with a positive attitude. It means finding joy in small moments and spreading that joy to others. It's about maintaining hope and optimism, no matter the circumstances.

Teaching your child to laugh and always smile is more than just a promotional strategy. It's a way of life that enhances well-being, builds strong social connections, and fosters a positive outlook. Smiling and laughing are tools that benefit you from the inside out, promoting health and happiness.

Incorporating these habits into your daily life and teaching them to your children creates a legacy of joy and positivity. You become a magnet, attracting others with your warmth and energy. Embrace the power of a smile and watch how it transforms your life and the lives of those around you. Always Be Smiling!

Please don't take my word for it. Here is part of my research on smiling, laughing, and their scientific benefits.

The Scientific Benefits of Laughter

Laughter is often considered the best medicine, and scientific research supports this age-old adage. Laughing triggers numerous physiological and psychological benefits that contribute to overall well-being. This chapter delves into the scientific benefits of laughter, highlighting case studies, clinical trials, and other research to underscore its importance.

Physiological Benefits

Laughter induces a physical response in the body, often described as a "laughter workout." When you laugh, several muscle groups in your face and body contract, increasing blood flow and oxygen intake and stimulating the heart and lungs. A study published in the *Journal of the American Medical Association* found that laughter could improve vascular function. Participants who watched a comedy show experienced improved blood vessel function and reduced arterial stiffness compared to those who watched a drama.

Hormonal Impact

Laughter significantly affects the endocrine system. It reduces levels of stress hormones such as cortisol and adrenaline while increasing the release of endorphins, the body's natural feel-good chemicals. This hormonal shift helps alleviate stress and promote a sense of well-being. A clinical study conducted at Loma Linda University showed that participants who watched humorous videos experienced a notable decrease in cortisol levels and an increase in endorphin levels.

Immune System Boost

Laughter can also enhance immune function. Research by Dr. Lee Berk at Loma Linda University demonstrated that laughter increases the production of antibodies and activates immune cells, such as T-cells and natural killer cells, which are crucial for maintaining health and combating disease. Participants in the study who engaged in laughter-inducing activities showed higher levels of these immune components compared to a control group.

Pain Management

The analgesic effect of laughter has been well-documented. Laughter triggers the release of endorphins, which are natural painkillers. A study published in *Proceedings of the Royal Society B* by researchers from the University of Oxford found that participants who watched 15 minutes of a comedy show could tolerate pain better than those who watched a documentary. This suggests that laughter can be an effective, natural pain management tool.

Psychological Benefits

Laughter profoundly impacts mental health by reducing anxiety and depression and enhancing mood. A case study involving elderly patients with depression found that those who participated in regular laughter therapy sessions reported significant improvements in mood and a decrease in depressive symptoms compared to those who did not. This study, published in *Geriatrics & Gerontology International*, underscores the potential of laughter as a therapeutic tool for mental health.

Social Bonding

Laughter plays a crucial role in social interactions and bonding. It creates a sense of connection and increases trust and empathy among individuals. Research from the University of Maryland showed that shared laughter enhances group cohesion and improves social bonds. This finding is supported by evolutionary theories suggesting that laughter has historically played a role in social bonding and group survival.

Longevity

There is also evidence to suggest that laughter can contribute to a longer life. A study conducted in Norway, known as the Norwegian HUNT study, followed over 53,000 participants for 15 years. It found that those with a strong sense of humor lived longer than those without. The researchers concluded that the health benefits of laughter and a positive outlook could extend life expectancy.

Keep Smiling

The scientific evidence is clear: laughter is a powerful tool for improving physical health, enhancing psychological well-being, and fostering social connections. From reducing stress hormones and boosting the immune system to managing pain and improving mood, the benefits of laughter are extensive and profound. Incorporating more laughter into your life can enhance your overall quality of life and well-being. So, make it a point to laugh often and share that laughter with others—your body and mind will thank you.

The Multifaceted Benefits of Laughter

Longevity

Physiological Benefits

Social Bonding

Hormonal Impact

Psychological Benefits

Immune System Boost

Pain Management

Figure 9 - Benefits of Laughter

Chapter 8
Law 3: The Law of Humility

Introduction to The Law of Humility

Humility can take many forms and have various interpretations. In karma, humility means accepting where you are right now. If a customer has a problem with your product or even with you, accepting the situation opens your karma, while arguing or defending your position subtracts karma.

Is it easy for you to stay quiet when someone criticizes you? For me, it's very challenging. Since childhood, I defended my position no matter what. If a coach corrected me, I would blame the other players. When I lost in public speaking contests, I blamed the judges. When a prospect didn't buy from me, I was devastated. I remember crying uncontrollably when we were disqualified from a big basketball tournament and wanting to throw my second-place speaking trophy after losing to a better speaker.

Humility Starts with Acceptance

Pay close attention to your employees, customers, and even your family. Identify when you accept situations and when you don't. Start working towards self-acceptance, bringing you closer to humility and positive karma.

Acceptance doesn't mean staying mediocre, not learning, or rejecting change. On the contrary, accepting where you are gives you a baseline to set goals and move forward. For example, if you want to do ten pull-ups but can only do two, acceptance means acknowledging your starting point and planning to improve incrementally.

In marketing karma, identify your monthly sales and your next step toward your goal. Break down your next step into the number of leads needed, how many of them are qualified, and how many prospects you need to close a single client. This gives you a numbers-based marketing plan that starts with humility and acceptance.

Acceptance can be difficult if you're a high achiever because high achievers constantly strive for improvement. But acceptance will actually help you grow. Being happy with who you are is vital to moving forward. For example, I was a basketball player growing up and the only one in varsity at sixteen. I played off the bench as a defensive player because my teammates were better scorers. However, I wanted to score, and I always left games disappointed with my performance.

Years later, while playing basketball for fun, my attitude changed. I was there to have fun, so I practiced differently. I accepted my abilities and focused on improving through specific drills. This acceptance and humility transformed my practice and performance. Eventually, I became a skilled shooter, enjoying the game more than ever.

Where do you show humility? What are your areas of opportunity? Write them down, and turn your opportunities into strengths.

Acceptance is a crucial component of growth.

The Law of Humility Summary

Marketing Karma Adaptation

Accepting your current market position and feedback from your audience allows for growth and improvement in your marketing strategies.

Introduction

The Law of Humility teaches that growth and improvement begin with acceptance. In marketing and business, this means accepting where you currently stand, understanding your strengths and weaknesses, and being open to feedback. By embracing humility, small business owners can identify areas for improvement, build stronger relationships with customers, and create a more authentic brand.

Understanding the Concept

The Law of Humility emphasizes self-awareness and acceptance. For business owners, this means acknowledging the reality of your current situation, being open to feedback, and recognizing that there is always room for improvement. Humility allows you to see your business from a broader perspective, helping you make better decisions and build a stronger foundation for growth.

Applying the Law to Your Business

1. **Self-Awareness:**
    - **SWOT Analysis:** Conduct a SWOT (Strengths, Weaknesses, Opportunities, Threats) analysis of your business. This helps you understand your current position and identify areas for growth. For example, a local bookstore might identify its strengths in community engagement, weaknesses in

online sales, opportunities in virtual events, and threats from larger online retailers.

- o **Reflective Practices:** Regularly take time to reflect on your business performance. What has worked well? What hasn't? This self-awareness helps you stay grounded and focused on continuous improvement.

2. **Customer Feedback:**

- o **Feedback Mechanisms:** Implement systems to collect customer feedback, such as surveys, reviews, and social media polls. Actively seek out and listen to this feedback. For example, a restaurant could use comment cards and online review platforms to gather customer opinions on their dining experience.
- o **Constructive Response:** Respond to feedback with humility and a willingness to improve. Thank customers for their input, address concerns, and take actionable steps to make necessary changes.

3. **Growth Mindset:**

- o **Continuous Learning:** Stay open to new ideas and opportunities for learning. Attend workshops, read industry publications, and engage with mentors. For instance, a graphic design freelancer might take online courses to stay updated with the latest design trends and software.
- o **Team Development:** Encourage a culture of humility and continuous improvement within your team. Provide opportunities for professional development and create an environment where feedback is valued and acted upon.

Examples of Small Business Owners

1. **The Humble Bakery:** Laura runs a small bakery known for its delicious pastries and warm atmosphere. Despite her success, Laura regularly asks her customers for feedback on new recipes and the overall experience at her bakery. She uses suggestion boxes and social media polls to gather opinions. When a customer mentioned that the seating area felt cramped, Laura took this feedback seriously and rearranged the layout to create a more comfortable space. This humble approach has improved her business and strengthened customer loyalty.

2. **The Reflective Consultant:** David is a marketing consultant who prides himself on delivering client results. He regularly conducts a SWOT analysis of his business to identify areas for improvement. When he realized his public speaking skills could improve, he enrolled in a communication course to enhance his abilities. David also asks his clients for feedback after every project and uses this input to refine his services. His humility and commitment to growth have made him a sought-after consultant in his field.

Key Takeaways

- Acceptance Leads to Growth: Embracing humility and accepting your current position allows continuous improvement.
- Value Feedback: Actively seek and respond to customer feedback to enhance your business.

- Cultivate a Growth Mindset: Stay open to new learning opportunities and encourage a culture of humility within your team.

Exercises

1. **Conduct a SWOT Analysis:**
   - Perform a SWOT analysis of your business. Identify your strengths, weaknesses, opportunities, and threats. Use this analysis to create an action plan for improvement.
2. **Implement Feedback Systems:**
   - Set up mechanisms to collect customer feedback. This could be through online surveys, comment cards, or social media interactions. Regularly review and act on this feedback.
3. **Reflective Practice:**
   - Schedule regular times for reflection. Consider what has worked well and what hasn't in your business operations. Use these reflections to make informed decisions.
4. **Professional Development Plan:**
   - Create a professional development plan for yourself and your team. Identify areas for growth and find relevant courses, workshops, or reading materials to enhance skills.

Conclusion

The Law of Humility emphasizes the importance of acceptance and self-awareness in achieving growth and improvement. By embracing humility, small business owners can better understand their current position, actively seek and respond to feedback, and foster a culture of continuous learning. These practices enhance business performance and build stronger, more authentic relationships with customers. Embrace the principles of Marketing Karma and let humility guide you toward sustained success.

Achieving Business Growth through Humility

Acceptance Leads to Growth

Value Feedback

Cultivate Growth Mindset

Figure 10 - Achieving Business Growth through Humility

Chapter 9
Law 4: The Law of Growth

Introduction to The Law of Growth

One of my favorite Buddhist sayings is, "If you want to make the world a better place, be happy because you're part of the world, and if you make yourself happy, you made the world better." If you want to provide extreme value to your clients, you need to be yourself of extreme value. That value comes with growth, and growth comes with investing time, money, and energy in yourself. Growth is not only about your mind and feelings; it's also about your body, appearance, vocabulary, and how you express yourself in person and in writing. Growth is about every part of who you are. Work on yourself, and karma will notice!

My Journey of Growth

I'm obsessed with growth, not because of karma. It all started when I was a teenager. I quickly realized I wasn't the smartest in my class—far from it. The kids were so bright that I knew I needed something else to get ahead, and it wouldn't be with my grades. I played to my strengths, focusing on subjects I excelled at, like astronomy, mythology, and poetry. At fifteen, I discovered influence and began studying influence, sales, and marketing. This is what you now know as marketing karma.

Influence and marketing were not the only things I studied. Over the years, I've delved into self-growth and personal development, martial arts, traveling, writing fiction and non-fiction, public speaking, mentoring, teaching, artificial intelligence, cognitive rehabilitation, and more.

Growth is not only about reading or learning. It includes digesting information and implementing it. I recommend teaching the information you learn as part of your self-growth process because if you can't teach it, you probably don't know it. Imagine starting as a young Kung Fu student at a Shaolin Buddhist temple in China. You learn, understand, practice, and fight. The real learning begins when you start teaching.

Fun Fact: In Kung Fu, a black belt means you master the basics.

Keys to Self-Growth

1. Learning
2. Digestion
3. Implementation

4. Teaching

You train your body and mind on new movements, ideas, concepts, and feelings by **learning**. You might apply the learning to your business with new products, discovering new markets, and keeping your mind open to new knowledge.

Digesting your newfound knowledge involves becoming mindful of the information, what to do with it, what it means, and learning from others' experiences and mishaps.

Implementation means applying your knowledge after you have fully digested it and understand how it works.

Teaching helps others understand and benefit from the knowledge. It puts you at another level of understanding because you don't know something until you can teach it.

Keys to Self-Growth

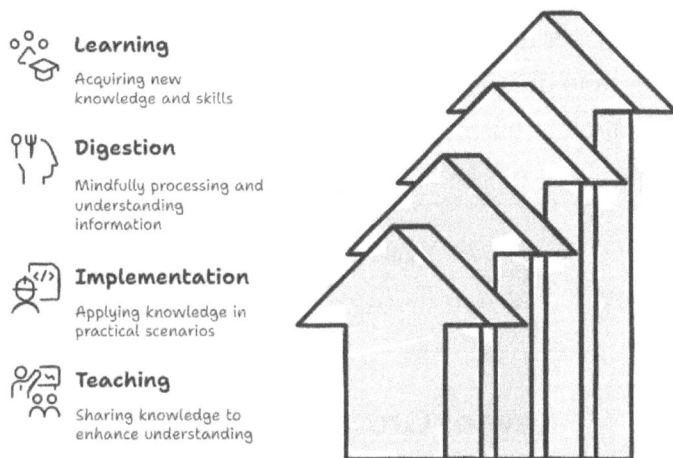

Learning
Acquiring new knowledge and skills

Digestion
Mindfully processing and understanding information

Implementation
Applying knowledge in practical scenarios

Teaching
Sharing knowledge to enhance understanding

Figure 11 - Keys to Self-Growth

My Martial Arts Journey

I've always loved martial arts and practiced several styles since childhood. I started Kung Fu a few years ago, specifically Choi Le Foot and Tai Chi. I fell in love with Tai Chi and eventually became a teacher. This is when I truly started learning Kung Fu. My previous training gave me a basic understanding, but teaching revealed how little I knew, especially about Tai Chi. It's one of the most challenging practices, testing your brain, body, and nerves, making you brighter from day one.

Business and marketing are more accessible to understand and apply than Tai Chi. You don't have to be an expert or a teacher in marketing to use it. The path might take weeks or months, but not years. With marketing, you only need to digest the information to understand how it applies to your business and how you can benefit from it.

To Provide Extreme Value, You
Need to Be Extremely Valuable.

Law of Growth Summary

Marketing Karma Adaptation

Personal and professional growth is essential for business success. Invest in self-development and encourage growth within your team.

Introduction

The Law of Growth underscores the importance of self-improvement and continuous learning. For small business owners, this principle emphasizes that real, lasting change starts from within. Entrepreneurs can enhance their skills, adapt to new challenges, and drive their businesses forward by focusing on personal and professional development. Encouraging growth within your team also leads to a more dynamic and resilient organization.

Understanding the Concept

The Law of Growth is based on the idea that to see external changes in our business and environment, we must first focus on internal changes. This involves self-awareness, a commitment to learning, and the willingness to step out of our comfort zones. In the business context, it means that as a leader, your personal growth will directly impact the development of your business. Moreover, fostering a culture of growth within your team can lead to innovative ideas and improved performance.

Applying the Law to Your Business

1. Self-Improvement:

- **Continuous Learning:** Commit to lifelong learning. This could involve reading books, attending seminars, or taking online courses relevant to your industry. For example, a small business owner in the tech industry might take coding classes or attend cybersecurity workshops to stay updated with the latest trends.
- **Mentorship and Coaching:** Seek out mentors who can provide guidance and perspective. Joining networking groups or professional associations can also provide valuable insights. For instance, an entrepreneur could join a local chamber of commerce or a business mastermind group.

2. Team Development:

- **Professional Development Programs:** Invest in training and development programs for your team. This could include workshops, certifications, or team-building activities. For example, a retail business might provide customer service training for their staff to improve the overall shopping experience.
- **Encouraging Innovation:** Create an environment where team members feel comfortable sharing ideas and taking risks. Regular brainstorming sessions and an open-door policy can foster creativity and innovation. For instance, a marketing agency might hold weekly idea sessions to generate fresh campaign concepts.

3. Adapting to Change:

- **Flexibility and Adaptability:** Be open to change and adapt your strategies. This includes staying attuned to market trends and customer feedback. A small restaurant, for instance, might adapt its menu based on customer preferences or seasonal ingredients.
- **Embracing Technology:** Utilize technology to streamline operations and enhance productivity. This could involve adopting new software, automating processes, or leveraging social media for marketing. For example, a local bookstore could implement an online ordering system and use social media to engage with customers.

Examples of Small Business Owners

Example 1: The Evolving Fitness Trainer

Jessica owns a small fitness studio. Recognizing the ever-changing nature of the fitness industry, she commits to continuous learning by attending fitness conferences and obtaining new certifications. She also encourages her trainers to pursue further education and offers incentives for completing advanced courses. Jessica's dedication to growth has allowed her studio to provide the latest fitness trends and techniques, attracting a diverse clientele and setting her business apart from competitors.

Example 2: The Adaptive Café Owner

Tom runs a cozy café in a busy neighborhood. He regularly seeks customer feedback and monitors industry trends to keep up with the evolving market. When he noticed a growing interest in plant-based diets, he took a course on vegan cooking and introduced a range of vegan options to his menu. He also invested in a digital loyalty program to engage with his customers better. Tom's willingness to adapt and grow has increased his customer base and enhanced customer satisfaction.

Key Takeaways

- **Personal Growth Drives Business Growth:** Continuous self-improvement drives business success.
- **Invest in Your Team:** Fostering a culture of growth within your team leads to innovation and improved performance.

- **Adapt and Evolve:** Stay flexible and open to change to remain competitive in a dynamic market.

The Law of Growth for Entrepreneurs

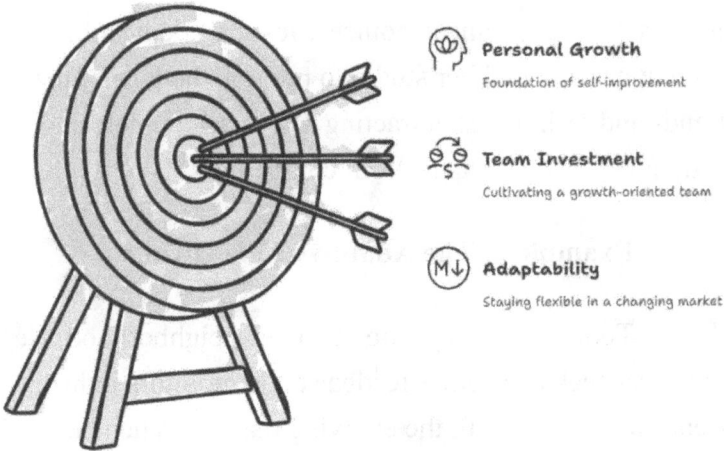

Personal Growth
Foundation of self-improvement

Team Investment
Cultivating a growth-oriented team

Adaptability
Staying flexible in a changing market

Figure 12 - The Law of Growth for Entrepreneurs

Exercises

1. Create a Personal Development Plan:

- Identify areas where you want to grow personally and professionally. Set specific, measurable goals and outline the steps needed to achieve them. For example, join a local Toastmasters club and attend monthly meetings to improve your public speaking skills.

2. Develop a Team Growth Strategy:

- Assess the current skills and development needs of your team. Create a training and development plan that includes workshops, courses, and team-building activities. Monitor progress and provide regular feedback.

3. Implement a Feedback System:

- Establish a system for regularly collecting and analyzing customer and employee feedback. Use this information to identify areas for improvement and implement changes as needed.

4. Stay Informed:

- Allocate time each week to stay updated with industry trends and news. Subscribe to relevant newsletters, follow industry leaders on social media, and participate in online forums and discussions.

Conclusion

The Law of Growth emphasizes the importance of continuous learning and self-improvement for business success. Small business owners can foster a dynamic and resilient business environment by focusing on personal development, investing in their team, and staying adaptable to change. Embrace the principles of Marketing Karma by prioritizing growth and learning, and watch your business thrive as a result.

Chapter 10
Inside-Out Promotions

Promote Yourself to Yourself

Self-promotion is only half the story; unselfishness is the other half, the Karma half. The way you leverage one with the other will start making sense soon if it doesn't already.

In this chapter, we'll talk about you and only you. I know there is a subtle change from the last chapters. This is still a book about self-promotion, influence, and marketing. So why are we promoting you to yourself? Simple: although we have ourselves on our minds most of the day, we often do so subconsciously. We're afraid of showing that we care for ourselves and others. We're so scared of being selfish.

Let's pause for a second and forget about the unselfish part of the book. Let's be a little selfish. Just a little! I don't mean selfish in a bad way, where we think only of ourselves and disregard everyone else. On the contrary, our selfishness will complement our "Unselfish Self Promotion" once we manage both properly.

Confused? Don't be. The concept is simple. You have to care about yourself. You are important—your passion, feelings, ideas, and attitude—all of these things matter. You are essential to your family, friends, and the world. You have something to say, something to add, something to contribute. You are critical. And now, after mastering the self-promotion tools, you can leverage your knowledge and importance. But before this happens, you must be important to yourself. You have to believe in yourself and believe you're important. You have to sell yourself to yourself. After all, if you don't wholly and sincerely believe you are important and worth self-promoting, nobody else will believe it either.

This doesn't sound very unselfish. Well, in reality, it is. If you are not at your peak performance, if you are not happy and healthy, how will you help others? It's challenging to think about and help others when feeling down, miserable, unhappy, or sick. When you're down, all you think about is yourself. When you're sick, you think about how to get healthier, take care of yourself, and be well again. So, learn to promote yourself.

Start from the beginning. It would help if you started your self-promotion from the beginning, and the beginning starts with you. The first step is to know yourself honestly. Think about what you want from life, from your self-promotion, not just what you want now, tomorrow, or next week. Don't just stop at figuring out what you want from work, or your kids, or your partner, but what you want—what you want.

You Should Be the Single Most Important Person to Yourself.

The Parent Trap

Parenting is an excellent example of how many people put themselves second or third in line regarding happiness, attention, and life in general. Once couples have children, life becomes all about the kids and less and less about themselves.

Attention all parents: if you are not happy and healthy in your own life, how do you expect to care for those around you who love you? You have to teach by example. Even if you don't think your kids can sense that you're not happy or healthy, you're wrong. They do know. They might not know how to express it, but they know.

Remember the quote, "Do as I do, not as I say"? Apply it here. Would you like your kids to be physically, mentally, and emotionally happy and healthy? Of course you do. So, teach them by example how to be happy. Let them see what it takes to live a happy and satisfying life. Let them see it from you.

What can you do? Think of yourself as an exact copy of what your children will be. You will always be on the right track if you have that picture. After all, they will be a lot like you, so don't screw it up!

To influence others, including your children, you have to influence yourself and believe in your influence. Kids are probably the most sensitive group of people. Even if they can't explain or rationalize it, they can feel it. So let them know how they can be happy and healthy. Start by showing them how to do it. They'll pick it up!

Let them be confident, like you. Let them know how they can be the best, like you. Let them change the world, starting with themselves. Show them how to be unselfish and share their happiness and health so they can make others healthy and happy.

Remember that your kids look up to you. They are following every one of your steps, so be wise and give them good examples. Show them with actions correctly, and remember that even the most minor details count.

Chapter 11
Law 5: The Law of Responsibility

The Law of Responsibility can be tricky, primarily because it prompts us to question: What is your responsibility? Are your children your responsibility? If so, to what extent? You need to feed them, but do you nourish their minds, souls, courage, and kindness? Do you let them be themselves, or do you try to mold them into what you desire?

Now, let's explore another challenging aspect: are your parents your responsibility? How about your siblings or cousins? Are your employees your responsibility?

In the realm of Karma, the answer is a resounding yes. Before you think, "But I have no time, money, or energy to deal with their life problems," let me ask you: What is life really about? Is it solely about your job and your business? Is it about your happiness? I believe not. Achieving personal happiness is relatively simple; ensuring everyone around you is happy is the real challenge.

Remember, everyone you're close to is your responsibility. Reflect on how you're fulfilling that responsibility, as your actions shape your karma.

Some responsibilities will come quickly, while others will be difficult. It's a process. You won't be able to change everything at once, but gradually, you can accept more responsibility, leading to greater rewards from karma.

I've had people living with me since childhood, and I still have family living with me now, which means they are my responsibility. I need to ensure they are fed, thrive in school, are happy, and have a plan. This is natural and easy for me, but I know it's not the same for everyone. Some of my friends can't host anyone, not even their parents. It can even lead to arguments with your spouse.

Karma Will Test You, or It Might Be God or Both

My first significant goal was to earn enough money so my mother and grandmother could retire. This drive led me to success, to become a VP, and soon after, a CEO in my late twenties. My goal wasn't to own a new car, better clothes, or more money but to retire my family to take responsibility for them as they had for me. This also had a karma payout because I reached my dreams. By twenty-nine, I had achieved all my lifelong goals and dreams because I embraced responsibility.

However, not everything was easy for me. I want to share a personal failure in my responsibility. Karma tests you, or it might be God or both! In my case, that responsibility involved my father and grandfather. Both were abusive husbands, and both my mom and grandma had to leave them, never receiving a nickel from them. I'm an only child, but my grandmother was alone with six kids. Can you imagine being a single mother in Tijuana? My grandmother was my best friend, and I adored her.

This story is about how I failed in my family responsibilities, especially as a grandson, blending Karma and Leadership, Karma Marketing, and Karma Leadership.

How Can You Use It?

This part of the Law of Responsibility, one of the laws of Karma, helps you understand how to use it in your life.

My Personal Story

It starts with my maternal grandfather. He abandoned my grandmother with six children. I never met or talked about him; he was taboo at home. I grew up with my grandmother, my best friend. One life goal was to retire my mother and grandmother from work. One day, I received a call from a town in central Mexico informing me that my grandfather, my mother's father, was sick and looking for her. At that time, I was already supporting my household financially. My mother, a very responsible person, flew out to rescue him despite my reservations.

We placed him in a nursing home in southern Mexico, paying all expenses. After a year, the house closed, and my mom moved him to another in Ensenada, closer to us. I feared this would upset my grandmother. Eventually, we rented him an apartment, but I never visited. None of my relatives did either. Despite taking financial responsibility, I failed emotionally. My grandfather, nearly blind and in a wheelchair, deserved compassion, but I remained distant, prioritizing my grandmother's feelings.

In hindsight, I realize I failed this test of Karma. I should have offered my grandfather love and understanding. His situation was a test of responsibility beyond finances—an emotional test I did not pass.

Applying the Law to Your Life

When faced with responsibility, it's easy to neglect it due to inconvenience. However, that's when Karma indeed appears, testing your resolve. Whether in business or personal life, your energy must be consistent. You cannot be one person in business and another in personal matters without deceiving yourself. This is not the path of Karma or self-improvement.

Summary: We Are Responsible for Our Lives.

Marketing Karma Adaptation

Take responsibility for your marketing actions and business outcomes. Own your successes and failures, and learn from them.

Introduction

The Law of Responsibility teaches that we are accountable for our actions and their outcomes. For small business owners, this principle emphasizes owning your marketing decisions and their impacts on your business. By accepting responsibility for successes and failures, you can learn valuable lessons, improve your strategies, and build a reputation for integrity and reliability.

Understanding the Concept

The Law of Responsibility is grounded in the idea that we are the primary agents of our fate. In a business context, this means that the outcomes of your marketing efforts—positive or negative—directly result from your actions and decisions. Embracing this responsibility empowers you to make proactive changes and continuously improve your business operations.

Applying the Law to Your Business

1. **Ownership of Actions:**

    o **Accountability:** Establish a culture of accountability within your business. Ensure that every team member understands their role and the impact of their actions. For instance, a small digital marketing agency might implement regular performance reviews to track progress and accountability.

    o **Transparency:** Be transparent with your customers and stakeholders about your business practices and decisions. This builds trust and credibility. For example, a local food delivery service could share its sourcing practices and environmental efforts with its customers.

2. **Learning from Failures:**

    o **Post-Mortem Analysis:** Conduct a thorough analysis of any marketing campaigns or business initiatives that did not meet expectations. Identify what went wrong and how you can avoid similar issues. A boutique clothing store, for instance, might review a failed product launch to understand why it didn't resonate with customers.

    o **Continuous Improvement:** Use failures as opportunities for growth. Implement changes based on the lessons learned to improve future performance. A coffee shop that receives negative feedback about its service might invest in customer service training for its staff.

3. **Celebrating Successes:**

   o **Recognize Achievements:** Acknowledge and celebrate your team's and your business's successes. This boosts morale and motivates further effort. A small tech startup could hold monthly meetings highlighting individual and team accomplishments.

   o **Share Success Stories:** Publicly share your success stories with your audience. This not only builds your brand's reputation but also demonstrates the effectiveness of your marketing strategies. A local bakery could share customer testimonials and success stories on social media.

Examples of Small Business Owners

- **The Accountable Hair Salon Owner:** Rachel owns a hair salon that prides itself on excellent customer service. Rachel took full responsibility when she started receiving complaints about long wait times. She implemented an online booking system and restructured staff schedules to manage appointments better. Rachel's transparency with her customers and proactive steps to address the issue resolved the problem and strengthened customer trust and loyalty.

- **The Reflective Marketing Consultant:** Ethan is a marketing consultant who values accountability. After a marketing campaign for a client did not perform as expected, Ethan conducted a detailed analysis to understand why. He discovered the target audience had been misidentified, and the messaging was off. Ethan took responsibility, explained the findings to his client, and revised the strategy. The following campaign was successful, thanks to the adjustments based on the lessons learned.

Key Takeaways

- **Embrace Accountability:** Taking responsibility for your actions and their outcomes leads to growth and improvement.
- **Learn from Failures:** Analyze failures to identify lessons and implement changes for better future performance.
- **Celebrate Successes:** Recognize and share your successes to build morale and demonstrate effectiveness.

Exercises

1. **Conduct a Post-Mortem Analysis:**
   - Select a recent marketing campaign or business initiative that did not meet expectations. Conduct a detailed analysis to identify what went wrong and how it can be improved. Document the findings and develop an action plan for future improvements.
2. **Implement an Accountability System:**
   - Establish a system for tracking accountability within your team. This could include regular performance reviews,

precise role definitions, and transparent communication channels. Ensure that everyone understands their responsibilities and the impact of their actions.

3. **Celebrate Successes:**
   - Create a plan to recognize and celebrate successes within your business regularly. This could involve monthly team meetings, social media shout-outs, or customer appreciation events. Highlight both individual and team accomplishments to boost morale.

4. **Share Your Story:**
   - Write a success story or case study about a recent achievement and share it with your audience. Use this opportunity to showcase your business's strengths and the effectiveness of your marketing strategies.

Conclusion

The Law of Responsibility emphasizes the importance of owning your actions and their outcomes in business. By embracing accountability, learning from failures, and celebrating successes, small business owners can continuously improve their operations and build a reputation for integrity and reliability. Implementing these practices enhances business performance and fosters more robust relationships with customers and stakeholders. Embrace the principles of Marketing Karma by taking responsibility for your business.

Want to Learn More?

- Book: "Extreme Ownership: How U.S. Navy SEALs Lead and Win" by Jocko Willink and Leif Babin

Figure 13 - The Law of Responsibility

Chapter 12
Black & White Marketing

Your Ethical Compass

"You Have a Responsibility to Your Customers."

Have you ever wondered what people say about you? What do people think of you? Would you like to influence their impressions of who you are and what you stand for? You can do it without telling them what to think or obsessing over it. There's a simple tool in your Marketing Toolbox designed for this. This tool will give people not just a first impression but "the impression"—a lasting, unchangeable perception that goes to the core of how people see you, what they think of you, and how they feel about you.

People must see you as fundamentally sound, not a saint, but a good person. Goodness can mean different things to different people, influenced by upbringing, religion, or education. Yet, there's often a lot of gray between good and evil, right?

This is the foundation of the Black & White promotional tool. Imagine making decisions with a Black & White mentality—no in-between, no gray areas. It's easy to understand but hard to apply. Predictable and reliable impressions require predictable and trustworthy behavior, as well as making consistent, transparent decisions.

Apply the Black & White tool to yourself, not others. Use it to guide your own actions, not to judge others. You can teach it to others, but avoid using it as a standard for others.

Living your life in black and white is tough. We face difficult situations daily, at work and with family and friends. Take a salesperson, for example, who might exaggerate product features or competitors' weaknesses. Are they lying? Probably not. Are they expressing an opinion? Probably. Is it Black or White? You decide. In your daily life, strive to make clear, ethical decisions. Distinguish between right and wrong and always choose the right path.

Black & White Habit

Let me share a secret I learned when I was younger that helps me make the right decisions, even when I'm not consciously thinking about it: Black & White is a habit.

The secret is my grandmother. She was the epitome of Black & White decision-making. I grew up close to her, a strong, hardworking woman who faced a tough life. She was left homeless twice with six children and raised them all to be honest, hardworking, Black & White decision-makers.

She taught me with actions, words, and examples. Her everyday life was a testament to Black & White decisions shared around the table over coffee and food.

So, what's the Black & White secret? Simple. I try to live my life as if my grandmother is watching. This perspective inspires me to act appropriately and live the right way, whether making small or large decisions. Find your inspiration and way of always making the Black & White decision.

Making Black & White decisions will leave a lasting stamp on you, your character, and everyone around you—family, employees, and colleagues. It's one of the best promotional activities you can ever practice. It's not short-term promotion; it's lifelong. Your Black & White example will outlive you, becoming a powerful Marketing Karma tool.

Developing a Strong Ethical Compass

Building a robust ethical compass is crucial for personal integrity and professional success. It serves as a guide in making decisions, ensuring that your actions align with your values and principles. Here's how you can develop a robust ethical compass:

1. Identify Your Core Values

- **Reflection**: Take time to reflect on what truly matters to you. Consider what you stand for and what principles you hold dear.
- **Prioritize**: Determine which values are non-negotiable. These principles will guide your decisions, even in challenging situations.

2. Educate Yourself

- **Ethical Frameworks**: Familiarize yourself with different moral theories and frameworks, such as utilitarianism, deontology, and virtue ethics. Understanding these can help you evaluate situations from various perspectives.
- **Historical Examples**: Study historical figures known for their ethical leadership. Learn from their successes and failures.

3. Seek Mentors and Role Models

- **Find Guides**: Identify individuals who exemplify ethical, solid behavior. They could be mentors, colleagues, or historical figures.

- **Learn from Them**: Observe how they handle ethical dilemmas and seek their advice when you face your own.

4. Practice Self-Awareness

- **Self-Reflection**: Regularly assess your actions and decisions. Ask yourself if they align with your core values and ethical principles.
- **Accountability**: Hold yourself accountable for your actions. Admit mistakes and learn from them.

5. Cultivate Empathy

- **Perspective-Taking**: Put yourself in others' shoes. Consider how your decisions and actions impact others.
- **Compassion**: Develop a genuine concern for the well-being of others. This will guide you to make decisions that are right for you and beneficial for those around you.

6. Establish Ethical Habits

- **Consistency**: Make ethical behavior a habit. Consistently apply your moral principles in all areas of your life, not just when convenient.
- **Routine**: Incorporate ethical decision-making into your daily routine. This can be through regular reflection, seeking feedback, and continuous learning.

7. Create an Ethical Environment

- **Surround yourself with Ethical People**: Build relationships with individuals who share your commitment to ethical behavior.
- **Encourage Ethical Behavior**: Foster an environment where ethical behavior is recognized and rewarded. This applies to both personal and professional settings.

8. Develop Ethical Decision-Making Skills

- **Evaluate Consequences**: Consider the short-term and long-term consequences of your decisions. How will they affect you and others?
- **Seek Input**: Don't make decisions in isolation. Seek input from others, especially those affected by your decision.
- **Weigh Options**: Consider all your options and choose the one that aligns best with your values and ethical principles.

9. Stay Informed

- **Continuous Learning**: Stay updated on ethical issues and debates in your field. Attend workshops, read books, and participate in discussions about ethics.
- **Critical Thinking**: Develop your ability to think critically about ethical issues. This will help you navigate complex situations with confidence.

10. Reflect on Outcomes

- **Analyze**: After making a decision, reflect on the outcome. Did it align with your ethical principles? What could you have done differently?

- **Learn**: Use these reflections to improve your future decision-making process.

Developing a strong ethical compass is an ongoing process. It requires reflection, education, and consistently applying your core values and principles. Following these steps ensures that your actions are guided by a solid ethical foundation, leading to personal integrity and professional success. Remember, a strong ethical compass benefits you and positively impacts those around you, creating a ripple effect of moral behavior.

Conclusion

Incorporating the Black & White tool into your life and business practices creates a clear, ethical foundation for your actions and decisions. It fosters trust and respect, building an unwavering and genuine reputation. This tool is about self-promotion through ethical consistency, providing a framework for making decisions that benefit you and inspire and uplift those around you. Embrace this tool, and you'll see how powerful and enduring ethical behavior can be in personal and professional realms.

"As you develop your personal brand for life, family, and marketing, let ethics be your compass."

Developing a Strong Ethical Compass

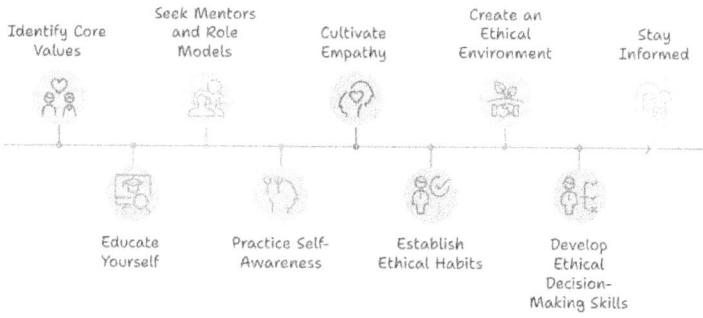

Identify Core Values

Seek Mentors and Role Models

Cultivate Empathy

Create an Ethical Environment

Stay Informed

Educate Yourself

Practice Self-Awareness

Establish Ethical Habits

Develop Ethical Decision-Making Skills

Figure 14 - Developing a Strong Ethical Compass

Chapter 13
Law 6: The Law of Connection

Introduction to The Law of Connection

When we discuss Karma or any concept from Eastern civilizations, we encounter a different feel to their principles. It's not just Karma; it's evident in mindfulness, spirituality, history, and religion. Oddly, the West has taken over three thousand five hundred years to catch up to the benefits of Eastern practices. For example, mindfulness meditation is now taught in neurology and psychology programs. Buddhist principles of forgiveness and staying in the present, avoiding focus on the past or future to prevent suffering, are also taught. Modern therapy often relies on these Buddhist principles.

After I suffered a terrible automobile collision that permanently injured my body and brain, I've been in cognitive and mental rehabilitation for seven years. It's incredible that most therapy is derived from Buddhist practices, including meditation, mindset changes, and exercises like Tai Chi and Yoga. I've consulted over ten neurologists, psychiatrists, and psychologists, all following a Buddhist playbook. Personal development coaches do the same, using Eastern principles.

Historically, the Western approach to problems was to tough it out and tackle them head-on. The approach is the opposite: focus on the present, accept problems as part of your reality, and get to know them instead of fighting them.

"You Are the Stuff of Stars!"

Growing up as an athlete and becoming an immigrant at eighteen, I knew best how to fight through problems. This approach worked until it didn't. At twenty, I realized that my stubborn personality wasn't effective. Fortunately, when the student is ready, the teacher appears. My uncle Miguel sat me down and explained how my attitude towards problems would affect my health in the long run. He challenged me to analyze my reactions to problems and find a permanent solution to my mindset, not just specific issues. Boom! My mind was blown. I realized I was the problem; the issues were just a matter of perspective. I took my uncle's challenge to heart and began a decade-long self-growth journey.

We Are the Same Stardust

Imagine the benefits of Eastern practices in place for two thousand years, now new to the West. Consider Marketing Karma: Karma first appeared in written form in 1500 BCE in the Rigveda, the oldest Hindu philosophy and religious text. Why has it taken so long for the West to apply these principles to our lives? Why aren't we using them in business and marketing? Well, we are now!

Part of the delay in adopting Eastern concepts was due to the lack of clinical studies, the basis of Western medicine and psychology. There's overwhelming evidence of the benefits of meditation, mindfulness, Tai Chi, and other Eastern practices. Some of these practices were seen as hocus pocus by the West, and some still are. For example, when I tell my students I meditate and practice Yoga and Tai Chi, they often ask, "Why?" This reaction surprised me, as I thought the benefits were self-evident.

Through chemistry, we learned that we're all made of the stuff of stars. The same hydrogen that burns in stars, bringing us light, food, and happiness, is around and within us. We share the same carbon, molecules, atoms, neutrons, and even quantum particles. Science now shows that quantum particles can communicate faster than the speed of light, suggesting a level of connectivity that defies current laws of physics. This means we're interconnected chemically, energetically, and communicatively in ways we've yet to understand fully.

While we won't use quantum mechanics in our marketing directly, we'll apply the principle of interconnectedness in Karma. Recognizing that everyone you serve is connected to you and fostering a kind heart and a business filled with positivity and goodness is what Marketing Karma is about.

Summary: Everything in the Universe is Interconnected.

Marketing Karma Adaptation

Recognize the interconnectedness of your marketing efforts. Consistent messaging and brand values across all platforms create a cohesive brand identity.

Introduction

The Law of Connection emphasizes that everything is interconnected. In business and marketing, this means that all your efforts—whether branding, customer service, or product development—are linked and contribute to the overall perception of your business. Understanding and leveraging this interconnectedness can lead to a more cohesive and powerful brand presence for small business owners.

Understanding the Concept

The Law of Connection is based on the principle that all system parts are interconnected. Your branding, messaging, customer interactions, and business practices work together in marketing to create a unified brand identity. A consistent and integrated approach ensures that every touchpoint with your customers reinforces your brand values and message, leading to stronger brand recognition and customer loyalty.

Applying the Law to Your Business

1. **Consistent Messaging:**

   o **Unified Brand Voice:** Develop a clear and consistent brand voice that reflects your business values and personality. Use this voice across all marketing channels, including your website, social media, and advertising. For example, a local craft brewery might use a friendly, casual tone that reflects its community-oriented ethos.

   o **Coherent Visual Identity:** Ensure your visual branding elements, such as logos, color schemes, and typography, are consistent across all platforms. This helps reinforce your brand identity and makes your business easily recognizable. A boutique clothing store, for instance, could use the same color palette and font styles in its signage, website, and social media posts.

2. **Integrated Marketing Efforts:**

   ○ **Cross-Channel Campaigns:** Plan and execute marketing campaigns spanning multiple channels, ensuring each platform supports the overall campaign message. To reach a wider audience, a small fitness studio could run a campaign promoting a new class using email newsletters, social media posts, in-studio posters, and local event sponsorships.
   ○ **Synergy Between Online and Offline:** Align your online and offline marketing efforts to create a seamless customer experience. For example, a bookstore might host in-store author readings and promote these events through its website and social media channels.

3. **Customer Experience:**

   ○ **Consistent Service Standards:** Ensure your customer service is consistent across all touchpoints, whether in-person, online, or over the phone. This builds trust and reliability. A small café could train its staff to provide the same friendly, attentive service in-store and during online interactions.
   ○ **Personalized Interactions:** Use customer data to provide customized experiences that reflect your understanding of their needs and

preferences. An online retail store could use purchase history and browsing data to recommend products tailored to individual customers.

Examples of Small Business Owners

Example 1: The Cohesive Coffee Shop Emma owns a coffee shop known for its cozy atmosphere and high-quality coffee. She ensures that her branding is consistent across all platforms, from the shop's rustic interior design to its website and social media presence. Her marketing campaigns, such as promoting a new seasonal drink, are integrated across email newsletters, Instagram posts, and in-store signage. Emma also provides a consistent customer experience by training her staff to deliver friendly and efficient service. This cohesive approach has built a strong brand identity and loyal customer base.

Example 2: The Integrated Health Coach Carlos is a health coach who provides personalized wellness programs. He maintains a consistent brand voice and visual identity across his website, social media, and printed materials. Carlos runs integrated marketing campaigns that include blog posts, webinars, and social media challenges, all centered around specific health topics. He also ensures that his customer interactions are consistent, whether through one-on-one coaching sessions or email correspondence. Carlos's commitment to a cohesive brand experience has attracted a dedicated following and increased client retention.

Key Takeaways

- **Consistency is Key:** A unified brand voice and visual identity across all platforms create a solid and recognizable brand presence.
- **Integrated Efforts:** Plan and execute marketing campaigns that leverage multiple channels for more significant impact.
- **Seamless Experience:** To build trust and loyalty, provide a consistent customer experience across all touchpoints.

Exercises

1. **Brand Audit:**
   - Conduct an audit of your current branding and marketing materials. Ensure your brand voice, visual identity, and messaging are consistent across all platforms. Identify any areas that need alignment and make the necessary adjustments.
2. **Integrated Campaign Planning:**
   - Plan a marketing campaign that spans multiple channels. Outline the critical message, target audience, and channels to be used. Ensure each platform supports the overall campaign and maintains a consistent message and visual identity.
3. **Customer Experience Mapping:**
   - Map out the customer journey from initial contact to post-purchase. Identify all the

touchpoints and ensure the experience is consistent and aligned with your brand values. Look for opportunities to personalize interactions based on customer data.

4. **Team Training:**
   o Train your team to understand and uphold the principles of consistent branding and customer service. Ensure that everyone knows your brand values and how to apply them in their interactions with customers.

Conclusion

The Law of Connection emphasizes the importance of recognizing and leveraging the interconnectedness of your marketing efforts. Small business owners can build a solid and cohesive brand identity by maintaining a consistent brand voice, integrating marketing campaigns across multiple channels, and ensuring a seamless customer experience. Embrace the principles of Marketing Karma by creating a unified and connected approach to your business, and you will see enhanced brand recognition and customer loyalty.

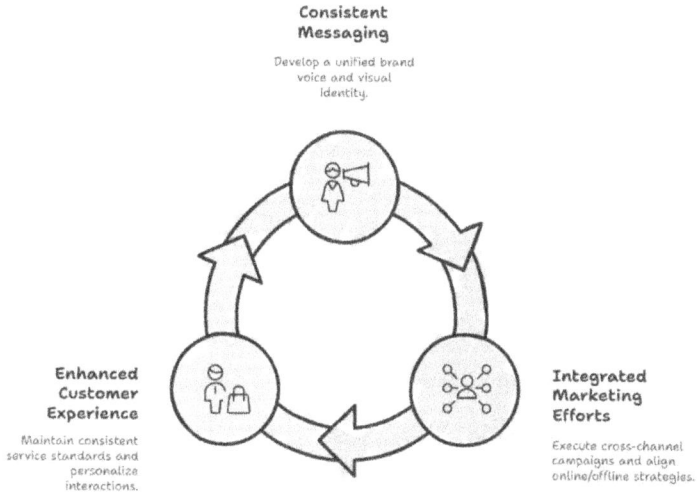

The Law of Connection in Branding

Consistent Messaging

Develop a unified brand voice and visual identity.

Enhanced Customer Experience

Maintain consistent service standards and personalize interactions.

Integrated Marketing Efforts

Execute cross-channel campaigns and align online/offline strategies.

Figure 15 - The Law of Connection in Branding

Chapter 14
The New Theory of Relativity

Einstein Has Nothing on You

Don't be intimidated by the title of this chapter. I'm not here to explain Einstein's theory of relativity. I remember struggling with Physics in school when I was fifteen. Einstein's theory was complicated to grasp then and hasn't gotten any easier. However, Einstein's core message was that we are all subject to the same universal laws. Isn't that profound? He wasn't talking about humanity or equality but something much grander—the universe itself. Nature behaves consistently on Earth, the moon, or another galaxy.

The New Theory of Relativity takes Einstein's philosophical principles and applies them to your life, thoughts, feelings, insecurities, and aspirations. It teaches us a simple lesson: everything is relative. Our problems, successes, mistakes, and feelings are all relative. Relative to what, you might ask? They are relative to everything else—other people's problems, feelings, or successes. If you have a significant problem, is it necessary only for you or everyone else? Does it matter to a war refugee in

Somalia or a starving child in Haiti? You see, it's all relative.

Many things are relative to points of view, especially when dealing with problems, politics, successes, failures, and even feelings. The importance of these issues lies in the attention we give them. It's all within our power of decision-making. We decide if a problem is big or small and how much attention we devote to it. It's your decision. You can make the problem big, small, or not even a problem, just an occurrence, a passage of time and space (back to Einstein!).

Imagine you and your spouse arrive at a shopping mall on the last day of Christmas shopping. You know you've left these last gifts until the end. The parking lot is packed, the stores are full, and shoppers are in a frenzy. What's your attitude? What do you think? I hope you're whistling and planning to have a good time. After all, you can't change the circumstances. It's the last shopping day, and you can't change the time. The mall is packed, and there's no parking; you can't change space. You can't return and shop in June for Christmas gifts.

Now that we've established your physical reality, what is your emotional reality? I hope you're happy and ready to have a good time hunting for the last Barbie, a large sweater, or the last copy of the hot video game. You can't control your space or time, but you can control your attitude and emotions. What about your spouse? Are you getting the same positive emotions? Or are you getting some nagging? Maybe you're the one nagging. "You always leave everything for the last moment," "You never plan ahead," "There is no parking," and "The mall will be too busy."

Here, you can apply The New Theory of Relativity immediately. It's the same mall, same parking lot, same car. Completely different emotions. What emotion do you choose to have? Which emotion do you choose to share? Think about it next time you're in a similar situation or the middle of a much bigger problem. Your reaction is not just affecting you and your spouse but your future. It's Karma at work.

Why is all this relativity essential for Marketing Karma? It's crucial because we're learning the ultimate type of promotion, Unselfish Self Promotion. To understand how promotion works, we need to know why people promote and what motivates them. Are people motivated by money? Acceptance? Power or fame? Survival? We must discover what drives people to promote themselves, what they promote, and why they do it. We must also put those needs and wants for promotion into a reality check. This is where the new theory of relativity comes in.

We all want to promote ourselves. We have a social instinct to survive and satisfy our needs. To do this, we promote ourselves. We do it as children by drawing attention, using tactics from tantrums to comedy. Think of a one-year-old boy who sees his mother caring for another baby. His first response is to get his mom's attention; his second is to cry or even act against the baby. Survival instincts in many mammals start with competing for food from the mother, pushing other siblings away. Puppies can die of malnutrition because they're too small to fight for their fair share of milk.

Our need for attention doesn't diminish as we grow older; we communicate it differently, even if we ask for it straight out: "I need some attention."

The New Theory of Relativity places our needs, wants, problems, and subsequent promotion in check. It lets us step back and see what we want to promote and why. It makes us think about our needs and wants to promote. Yes, it's self-awareness and mindfulness.

The New Theory of Relativity also gives us a reality check. It forces us to look at our lives, relationships, and problems and compare them to the rest of the world's issues. After this comparison, we can re-evaluate our lives, relationships, and problems and ask ourselves, "How are they related to the rest of the population? Are they so dreadful? Can we fix them? Will we give them a high level of importance and attention, or focus on something else, something more important?"

The Two Laws in The New Theory of Relativity

1. Our Problems Are Relative to Other People's Problems
2. Our Problems Are Relative to the Importance We Give Them (Our Ego!)

To Whom It May Concern

We live our lives thinking primarily of ourselves. We prefer to focus on our problems, reality, family, feelings, money, needs, and wants. Pay attention to how often you think about yourself daily. You're hungry, thirsty, sad, tired, missing someone, needing a vacation, unsatisfied at work, sick, or lonely. We're very concerned with ourselves. We're even obsessed. We even think of ourselves when someone else does something we don't like. "You're dropping out of school? How can you do this to me?" you might tell your kids.

Our self-obsession is part of our self-preservation and is wired into our system. Even when we think of someone else, like our parents, kids, friends, or spouse, we think of them or worry about them as they relate to us. After all, if we're not here, we wouldn't worry! Let's go a step deeper. If someone dies, we feel grief. The grief we feel is an absence, a void in our existence, day, and life.

That feeling is egocentricity. It's a feeling created by the effect death has on us. It's always about us.

Now that you know this and that you and everyone else are like this, let's take the attention away from us and place it on someone else. This is how we start changing our Marketing Karma.

By realizing what is important to us and how we think and act, we gain insight into what is important to others, how they feel and act, and what motivates them to act, react, or do certain things. We will see the world from the other person's point of view. This is the first part of Marketing Karma.

Marketing Karma starts by understanding our needs and wants and how we react to them, then learning how others do the same.

The 1st New Law - Relativity in The World

A seasoned executive in California worries about getting a big promotion: a Vice President position, a raise, and a bonus. At the same time, a young mother in Africa worries about what to feed her malnourished two-month-old baby to prevent another death.

Though their realities differ, their needs, wants, problems, and feelings are similar. They are both consumed by their problems. While the executive's problem might seem insignificant compared to a child's life, it's the most crucial issue in his life. It's all relative!

This is the first lesson in the New Theory of Relativity. Our problems are relative to other people's problems. When faced with everyday difficulties, always remember the first law of this new theory.

We all know that others need us and that wars, starvation, and suffering exist around the planet. We know some people struggle with drug habits, loneliness, homelessness, and immense troubles.

Once you finish reading this book and become a Marketing Karma machine, I'll ask you to promote for those in need. That's all it takes to change the world—one person at a time.

The 2nd New Law - It's All in Your Head

This is the story of two very different people, separated by geography: one lives in a third-world country, Mexico, and the other in the most powerful nation in the world, the USA. This is the story of how geography placed them in different realities they couldn't control. This is the story of two boys.

We can't control where we are born. If we're born in Africa or another part of the world that suffers from malnutrition, war, or natural disasters, with not enough to eat, no clothes, no house, no running water, that's just the luck of the draw. Conversely, being born in first-world countries, or at least not into starvation, is also luck. The following are two real stories of two real boys. We'll see not only their experiences and realities but also how they view them, how they feel about their circumstances, and why.

3rd World Luck

The first boy was born in a third-world country to a single mother—a familiar story for many. He was an only child in a lower-class neighborhood without running water or electricity. Since age nine, he had to carry buckets of water from the nearest source, about 300 feet from his house, up and down a flight of fragile stairs. No running water meant no shower, and without a water heater, he had to heat water in buckets to bathe.

Without electricity, his family used candles at night and sometimes petroleum lamps. He had to walk half a mile to buy petroleum and carry it home. TV and radio were nonexistent, and they had a cooler with ice to keep some food and drinks. He was mainly alone as his mother worked full-time to pay the bills, but he managed to stay out of trouble for the most part.

The boy walked two miles to school and back every day. The roads were unpaved, and he had to trudge through the mud during the winter rains. His shoes were caked in mud, which hardened and peeled off, leaving a mess around his desk. The other boys made fun of him, and the teacher scolded him. During recess, he tried to clean up his mess.

There were no luxuries in this boy's life, only the bare essentials to survive. At first glance, it seems he wasn't born happy, healthy, or wealthy.

Born With a Silver Spoon

The second boy lived a different life. This boy lived in the USA, went to the best private schools, had the best education money could buy, played sports, participated in extracurricular activities, went on family vacations, and lived in a family-owned home. He had a large support circle involved in his life, well-being, and future.

This boy seemed happy, healthy, and wealthy, and his life continued like this. But was he really born that way?

So, What's the Catch?

I know you've only read a few pages of my book, and we're just getting to know each other. This story has a catch, as with many of my stories. This is why the 2nd Law of the New Theory of Relativity is called "It's all in your head." Perception greatly influences reality and relativity. How you see the world, your life, your happiness, or the cards dealt to you depends on your perspective. It's all in your head!

So, what's the catch? Is there a catch to the story? Yes, the two boys are the same person. The two boys mentioned above are really me. How can that be? It's simple; just read between the lines. I live in the USA, in sunny San Diego, California, but I was born in Mexico, a third-world country. It's true I didn't have electricity or running water growing up and had to carry buckets of water up to three times daily, and I have a bad back to prove it! Later, my mother bought a house, but we couldn't afford electricity, running water, or a sewer system until I was out of high school. After landing my first job, I installed hot water after college and finished paying for our mobile home.

Yes, it's also true I went to one of the best Catholic private schools in Tijuana. My mother worked hard to pay for it. Maybe that's why we couldn't afford electricity or running water. Later, I enrolled in college in San Diego. It was a two-hour commute to school, and I didn't have a car. I used public transportation and sometimes didn't have money for the ride back. I had to hitch a ride or ask for bus money. I even slept on campus a couple of times, but that's a story for another day.

Now you see how I got to this chapter and its name. It was out of personal experience. Back then, I was happy. I don't remember ever being unhappy, even though I didn't have money, a car, or running water. This is why I say it's all in your head. You must take what you have and see it as the raw materials to build something else. And always remember, you will find happiness in the building process, not when you're done building.

Find your story, inspiration, mission, raw materials, and project, and promote unselfishly.

Reality Check Exercises:

Next time you have a problem, an argument, or feel blue, go through some questions to put your situation into perspective and think. It's all relative!

- How are my problems related to the rest of the population?
- How are my problems related to someone in Somalia?
- Are my problems so dreadful? Do they have solutions?
- How does my ego play into these problems or feelings?
- If I remove self-pity, would it fix the problem or feeling?

How should I approach my problems to gain perspective?

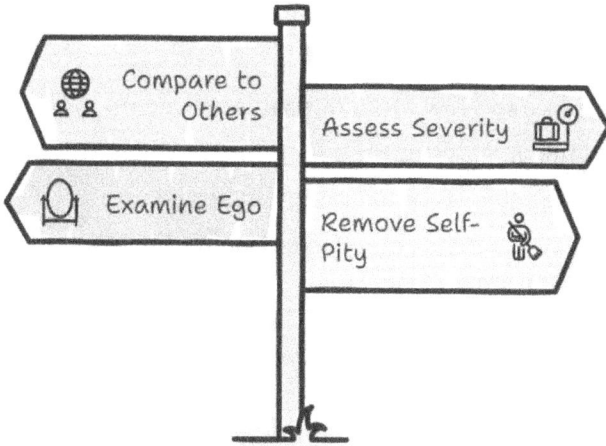

Figure 16 - Gain Perspective on Your Problems

Chapter 15
Caveman Promotion

Marketing Karma for Self-Preservation

I like to view modern problems and opportunities through the lens of our prehistoric ancestors. Consider this: modern humans like you and me, with the same intelligence and emotions, have been on this planet for around 250,000 years. Of those, we've been in a modern religious era in the West for about two thousand years, and it's only been about fifty years since most of humanity could read and write. Historical records have existed for less than five thousand years. So, what did we do for the other 95% of our existence? Those were our cave years.

I use the term "Caveman" to represent the entire prehistory period, which spans much longer than our time in caves. We probably spent more time in trees than caves, but "three humans" don't have the same ring.

As cavemen or cavewomen, the primary goal was simple: do anything to survive! Survival involves basic physiological needs: breathing, food, water, sex, sleep, and homeostasis. These needs are at the very bottom of Maslow's Pyramid of Needs. The pyramid illustrates that we must fulfill our basic needs before we can concern ourselves with higher pursuits like philosophy, art, or charity. Basic survival needs include not getting eaten by a tiger.

The need to survive pushed cavemen towards self-promotion or self-preservation. This was driven by the realization that survival becomes more manageable when working as a team. This includes hunting, gathering, building shelter, starting fires, or protecting against predators.

Imagine discovering the concept of team survival for the first time. What would you do if you knew your survival depended on the survival of others—your group, family, or clan? If one or more members of the team perish, get eaten by a predator, or starve, you could be next. Your food and protection depend on the group.

Picture cavemen working instinctively as a team, a clan, a society. Hunting parties of five or ten men go out together. Some women gather roots and fruits while others watch over the children and stay alert for predators. Everyone shares food, protects each other, and realizes that group self-preservation is easier. If the group doesn't survive, neither do you.

One of the Best Motivators of Marketing Karma is Self-Preservation

There's a natural instinct to socialize and coexist with others. However, exploiting this social habit is hard when your life is on the line. Survival comes first!

In the process of survival, cavemen and cavewomen needed each other. This "need" for others forced them to ensure their companions were happy, protected, well-fed, and prosperous. Cavemen cared about others because others were essential to their survival.

"Substitute Caveman and Cavewoman with YOU, and Self-Preservation with Marketing Karma."

Like the caveman, we must realize that others are crucial for our survival. We no longer need to work with others to hunt or fend off predators. In first-world countries, we don't need others for basic survival, but we do need others to supercharge our self-promotion.

Yes, we can achieve a lot on our own with hard work and passion. But if we also care about others and their promotion, they will likely promote us in return. This is true in politics, business, and family. The cavemen's lessons have been forgotten by many, but not by you. You will always help your fellow cavemen (just don't call them cavemen). Caveman Promotion delves into the heart of Marketing Karma. It presents a stripped-down, back-to-basics view of self-promotion, reframed as self-preservation. That's a powerful motivation to work with others, to help others survive and prosper.

Applying Caveman Lessons to Modern Life

Jump ahead a few thousand years to our current reality. You don't need to hunt, watch out for tigers, or dig up your own food. How can you use the lessons of the cavemen in your daily life and your marketing karma? Apply the same principles as if you were a caveman. Promote others with passion. Look out for their interests and happiness as if your life depended on it. Once you do this, you will have mastered the core of Marketing Karma.

I wrote the book "Nace Un Gigante De Un Emprendedor Cavernicola" in Spanish ("Caveman Entrepreneur") to highlight the importance of shifting from employee to entrepreneur, returning to what humans are naturally inclined to do.

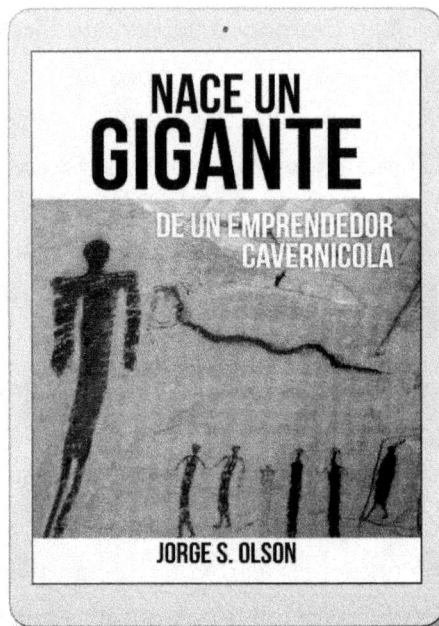

Figure 17 - "Nace Un Gigante" Book

Chapter 16
Listening Karma

Your Sales Secret Weapon

I've often heard that people who talk a lot are perceived as good salespeople. Maybe it's because they come across as fast-talkers or seem adept at convincing and persuading towards a purchase.

It could also be that these people are naturally sociable and enjoy talking—not just in business but in general. They easily chat with friends, family, and even strangers.

Another reason might be that these "talkers" are visual people. They see the world in pictures, photographs, or even high-speed video. Visual people tend to speak more and faster because they need to describe their mental images in detail. Imagine trying to explain a movie while it's playing. You'd have to talk a lot to keep up.

"Listening Makes You Likable!"

Talking is Not Selling

Next time you observe a "fast-talking salesperson," delve deeper into the conversation. You'll probably find that this person is visual and very friendly.

I mentioned earlier that you don't have to be highly extroverted to be an excellent self-promoter. You don't have to be a talker either. On the contrary, if you are a "fast-talking extrovert," you must learn to channel that energy into the right kind of talking—and even more into listening.

The Benefits of Listening

Listening has two crucial by-products: Marketing Karma and Learning. Even without the Marketing Karma, listening is a valuable skill to master. It starts with just listening and later evolves into asking questions and "getting" people to open up. You don't just want superficial conversations. The secret to perfecting your listening skills is simple: shut up.

My grandmother always said, "It is hard to learn with your mouth open." In other words, shut up and listen.

A By-product of Listening is Learning

Listening and not talking takes practice. We are selfish by nature; we think our point of view is interesting, important, insightful, or even brilliant. Often, we want to interrupt the other person or "jump in" in the middle of an idea or sentence to give our opinion.

Action Items

Start to listen, deeply listen. Do not interrupt your spouse, kids, parents, or family members. It isn't polite and usually turns off the person speaking to you. In the future, they won't come to you when they need to talk and be heard.

Do you feel the urge to give your excuse for why something went wrong before they even finish telling you it was wrong? Don't! Don't assume you know what the other person is going to say.

Do you jump in with your comments while others are finishing their sentences? Don't! We all feel the urge to jump in, interrupt, and talk about what we think, do, and feel. But resist this urge, and you'll see the other person appreciate it and return to you when they need to be heard.

Don't make others feel they don't know what they're discussing. Participate but not in a corrective way. Don't discredit people's ideas and points of view. Be a respectful and considerate listener.

Advanced Listening Strategies

It's important to listen deeply and relate this information to the person speaking, not to you. What do I mean? Don't try to apply everything to how it affects you or how you feel. Relate it to the speaker and how they are feeling and thinking. Let's call this listening "Advanced Listening."

Advanced Listening means removing selfishness from the equation. It means listening to learn from the other person, offering advice, a solution, or sympathy, getting to know them, or helping them. Note that you don't always have to solve problems; sometimes, listening means listening!

A key element in truly listening is eye contact. There's nothing more reassuring than having your listener look you directly in the eye. It shows that they have your undivided attention and that what they say is important to you. Don't look distracted. Don't look at your watch, phone, or someone passing by. If you do, the person speaking may stop until they capture your attention again.

Remember, you don't have to provide a solution to every conversation. This is especially true for personal, non-business relationships. For all the men reading this book, don't try to "talk" and solve all problems when your daughter, wife, mother, or sister is venting or speaking with you. Listen! If they want your advice, input, or solutions, they will ask for it.

The Right Time and Place

It's as essential to know when and where to listen as it is to understand how to listen. Don't push others to speak with you; don't try to get information from them. There's timing to the listening equation. Don't force others to speak when you're ready to listen. They won't want to talk if they're not ready, are busy, or have their mind elsewhere, even if you're prepared to listen.

Avoid simple mistakes like standing next to someone waiting for them to get off the phone to have a meaningful conversation or asking your spouse or kids to turn off the television "this instant" because you want to speak now. Wait for the right time. Be patient. Don't get mad or aggressive. Listen. They will know you are listening because you are an unselfish self-promoter and have already proven that you are there to help them and others.

In addition to timing, there's also a place to listen. You're often ready to listen, but the other isn't ready to talk. It's not good timing or simply not the right place. Don't try to understand precisely why everyone has different ways of expressing themselves or why they want to speak in some situations and not in others. Part of listening is accepting how people are, and if they're uncomfortable, you must respect it, not analyze it and try to convince them.

Me vs. You: Shift Your Focus

Can you stop talking about you, your company, and your products?

The most overlooked and understated rule in sales is the "Me vs. You" rule. For every time you use the words "me," "my," "I," "our," or "we," you should use "you" or "your" at least twice as often. For example, instead of saying, "My product, my company, my idea, I do this, our price, our benefits, our points," you should be saying, "Your benefits, your solutions, your price, you will profit," etc.

This applies to sales presentations, letters, statements, and even conversations. Pay close attention to the email or letter you write and see if you follow this rule. Why is this important? It's not just about how many times you use a word. It shows the buyer you care about them, their problems, their company, and their solution.

Are they buying your product simply because of the product or because of what it will do for them? When you are selling yourself, not a product or service, you start using the right tools—the Marketing Karma Tools. The moment you think you're selling a product or a service, you fall into the "me" trap. You're selling yourself as someone who will look out for the customer in any situation, with any product. Your goal is for them to trust you completely, to call you when they need something, to have you on speed dial, to follow you on social media, and to recommend you to their friends.

Consultative Listening: A Higher Level of Engagement

Business consultants have known for years that many answers to important questions and even solutions are within a business organization, within their employees, management, suppliers, and customers. Many employees within organizations don't think consultants do a great job because they believe consultants are given a list of problems and solutions and then turn around and present them to management logically.

Consultative Selling is not just for selling consulting. It's a sales technique that makes the salesperson into the consultant. Instead of just selling, the salesperson listens and comes up with solutions for the client. These salespeople make the most money, are well-trained, and are in high demand.

In Consultative Listening, you ask vital questions to employees, managers, suppliers, and customers. Essentially, you're listening. You must be a great listener and ask key questions. You sit down with each individual and ask them what they do, how they do it, and how they interact with colleagues, suppliers, customers, and other stakeholders. You ask about their job, their problems, what works, what doesn't, and you ask for solutions. From the outside, it's elementary. You get all the answers and then come back with the best solutions, often the exact solutions provided by the employees initially. Again, it looks basic in theory, but in practice, it's not. You're dealing with many people, some employees and some not, who may think they will lose their job, don't want to tell you what they do because they fear being replaced, or are simply afraid or angry.

A great Consultative Listener can put you at ease and make you feel unthreatened, like a friend. Furthermore, a Consultative Listener can take basic questions and get amazing answers. People don't always give you the best and most potent answer the first time around. They don't know what you're looking for; you probably didn't ask the right questions. If you ask, "What do you do in the company?" you'll likely get a very general answer like "I'm an accountant" or "I'm the warehouse manager."

Listening and Marketing Karma

Listening is at the heart of Marketing Karma. When you listen, you share your time, attention, and emotions. This unselfish act builds a bridge of trust and understanding. Whether in business or personal life, effective listening can transform relationships and open doors to opportunities.

Consultative Listening in Practice

Business consultants have known for years that many answers to important questions and even solutions are within a business organization, within their employees, management, suppliers, and customers. Many employees within organizations don't think consultants do a great job because they believe consultants are given a list of problems and solutions and then turn around and present them to management logically.

Consultative Selling is not just for selling consulting. It's a sales technique that makes the salesperson into the consultant. Instead of just selling, the salesperson listens and comes up with solutions for the client. These salespeople make the most money, are well-trained, and are in high demand.

In Consultative Listening, you ask critical questions to employees, managers, suppliers, and customers.

Essentially, you're listening. You must be a great listener and ask key questions. You sit down with each individual and ask them what they do, how they do it, and how they interact with colleagues, suppliers, customers, and other stakeholders. You ask about their job, their problems, what works, what doesn't, and you ask for solutions. From the outside, it's fundamental. You get all the answers and then come back with the best solutions, often the exact solutions provided by the employees initially. Again, it looks basic in theory, but in practice, it's not. You're dealing with many people, some employees and some not, who may think they will lose their job, don't want to tell you what they do because they fear being replaced, or are simply afraid or angry.

A great Consultative Listener can put you at ease and make you feel unthreatened, like a friend. Furthermore, a Consultative Listener can take basic questions and get amazing answers. People don't always give you the best and most potent answer the first time around. They don't know what you're looking for; you probably didn't ask the right questions. If you ask, "What do you do in the company?" you'll likely get a very general answer like "I'm an accountant" or "I'm the warehouse manager." That's not your desired answer, so you better ask different, more specific questions. You need to know the relationships this person has with others, not just what they do or the steps they take to do it.

Active Listening Do's and Don'ts:

Don'ts:

- Don't cross your arms
- Don't get angry
- Don't overreact
- Don't judge
- Don't interrupt
- Don't share your own story

Do's:

- Control your expressions
- Ask questions
- Always be there
- Be relatable
- Look them in the eyes
- Make them feel comfortable
- Use consultative listening

Active Listening Do's and Don'ts

Pros	vs	Cons
Control expressions		Cross arms
Ask questions		Get angry
Be present		Overreact
Be relatable		Judge
Maintain eye contact		Interrupt

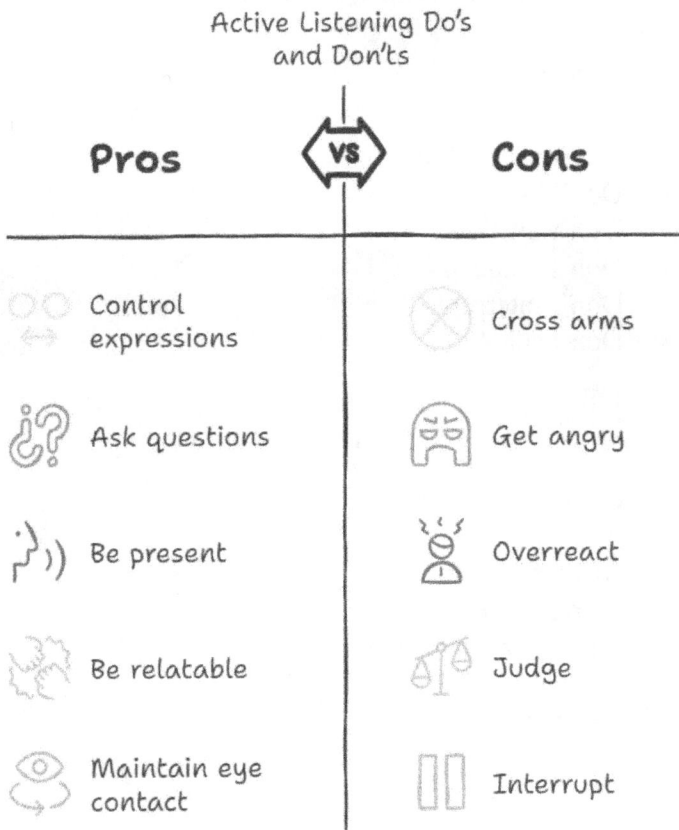

Figure 18 - Active Listening Do's and Don'ts

Listening: The Path to Influence

Influence is not about talking; it's about listening. When you listen, you gain insights into what matters to others. This knowledge allows you to tailor your interactions to meet their needs and expectations. Listening

182

is your most powerful tool, whether you're trying to sell a product, build a relationship, or lead a team.

In Marketing Karma, listening is the foundation upon which all other strategies are built. It is through listening that you understand the desires, fears, and motivations of others. This understanding enables you to connect with them more profoundly, fostering trust and loyalty.

Practical Steps to Improve Your Listening Skills

1. **Be Present**: Give your full attention to the person speaking. Avoid distractions such as phones or other people.
2. **Show Interest**: Nod, smile, and use verbal acknowledgments like "I see" or "That makes sense."
3. **Avoid Interrupting**: Let the speaker finish their thoughts before you respond.
4. **Ask Open-Ended Questions**: Encourage deeper conversation by asking questions that require more than a yes or no answer.
5. **Paraphrase and Reflect**: Repeat what you've heard in your own words to show that you understand and clarify any misunderstandings.
6. **Practice Empathy**: Try to understand the speaker's perspective and feelings.

Step-by-Step Consultative Sales

Consultative listening is more than just hearing words; it's about understanding their profound meaning. It's a crucial skill for anyone looking to build strong relationships, whether in business or personal life. Here's how you can apply consultative listening effectively:

1. Prepare to Listen

Before engaging in a conversation, prepare yourself mentally. Clear your mind of distractions and be ready to focus entirely on the person speaking. This shows respect and demonstrates that you value their time and words.

Action Tip: Take a few deep breaths and set an intention to listen actively before starting the conversation.

2. Create a Comfortable Environment

Ensure the setting is conducive to a good conversation. Choose a quiet place where you won't be interrupted, and ensure the person feels comfortable and at ease.

Action Tip: Arrange meetings in a quiet office or a cozy café with minimal distractions.

3. Ask Open-Ended Questions

Encourage the speaker to share more by asking open-ended questions. These questions can't be answered with a simple "yes" or "no" and invite the person to elaborate.

Example:

- Instead of asking, "Did you like the meeting?" ask, "What did you think about the meeting?"

4. Use Paraphrasing and Reflecting

Show that you are actively listening by paraphrasing what the speaker has said and reflecting it to them. This confirms your understanding and allows the speaker to correct any misinterpretations.

Example:

- Speaker: "I've been feeling overwhelmed with the new project."
- You: "It sounds like the new project has been quite challenging for you. Can you tell me more about what's been overwhelming?"

5. Observe Non-Verbal Cues

Pay attention to the speaker's body language, facial expressions, and tone of voice. Non-verbal cues can provide significant insights into their true feelings and thoughts.

Action Tip: Notice if they seem nervous, excited, or hesitant, and respond appropriately to these cues.

6. Provide Feedback

Give thoughtful feedback that shows you've listened and understood. This can be as simple as nodding or saying, "I understand." More detailed feedback might involve summarizing key points or expressing empathy.

Example:

- "I can see why you'd feel that way. It must be tough to manage all those responsibilities."

7. Avoid Interrupting

Let the speaker finish their thoughts before you respond. Interrupting can disrupt their train of thought and make them feel undervalued.

Action Tip: If you have a thought while they're speaking, jot it down quickly to remember later rather than interrupting.

8. Ask Follow-Up Questions

After the speaker has finished a point, ask follow-up questions to dig deeper. This shows that you are engaged and interested in their perspective.

Example:

- "Can you explain how this issue affects your daily workflow?"

9. Summarize and Confirm

At the end of the conversation, summarize the main points and confirm with the speaker to ensure you've understood correctly.

Example:

- "So, I'm hearing that the main challenges are time management and resource allocation. Is that correct?"

10. Show Empathy and Understanding

Demonstrate empathy by acknowledging the speaker's feelings and experiences. This builds trust and strengthens your relationship.

Example:

- "I can imagine how frustrating that must be. It sounds like you've been handling it as best as possible."

Practical Application in Different Scenarios

In Business:

- **Client Meetings**: Use consultative listening to understand the client's needs and challenges before proposing solutions. This builds trust and shows that you are genuinely interested in helping them succeed.
- **Team Management**: Listen to your team members to understand their concerns and ideas. This fosters a collaborative environment and encourages innovation.

In Personal Life:

- **Family Conversations**: Apply these techniques to understand your family members' perspectives and strengthen relationships.
- **Friendships**: Use consultative listening to support your friends through their challenges and celebrate their successes.

Conclusion

Consultative listening is a powerful tool that goes beyond essential communication. It involves active engagement, empathy, and a genuine interest in understanding others. Mastering this skill can enhance your personal and professional relationships, making you a more effective leader, friend, and partner. Remember, the key to successful listening is to focus on the speaker, understand their needs, and respond thoughtfully.

Chapter 17
Law 7: The Law of Focus

Introduction to The Law of Focus

I used to think I was an excellent multitasker until my neurologist told me the brain could only focus on one thing at a time. What we call multitasking is just the brain switching quickly between tasks. In Marketing Karma, as in all business, focus is crucial. Without it, you'll jump from one task to the next without achieving meaningful goals.

The Challenge of Focus

This is a tough pill for me to swallow, as I'm constantly juggling multiple projects, reading several books, and even writing numerous books simultaneously. While these activities can be beneficial, you still need the ability to focus on demand, finish tasks, and see marketing projects through to completion. In Marketing Karma, this means starting a marketing funnel and seeing it through to monetization before moving on to the next strategy, tip, or trick. Information is essential, but after you digest it, it's time to focus, take action, and implement your marketing strategy to get leads, prospects, and sales.

"When you focus on one marketing strategy—the one that will generate revenue—you'll see other aspects of your life come into focus, not just in business but in your personal life too."

Executives and Entrepreneurs Need to Focus

Executives and entrepreneurs need a clear, focused plan they can follow and check daily. Knowing what you need to do each day, instead of starting with emails or busy work, is essential. The same applies to your employees. Without a focused plan, they'll wander and engage in activities that don't generate revenue. So, focus on yourself and your company.

When I was a kid, there were no learning disabilities. You were either smart or dumb, distracted, or a bad student. If you couldn't focus the way your teacher wanted, you suffered. Now, we know that people learn and focus differently. It's not black and white, so discover how you focus best.

"I struggle both with focusing and stopping my focus. It's strange, but I find it difficult to concentrate on one thing; I want to focus on ten things at once."

Discover Your Focus Style

Do you have OCD or ADHD? Find the best ways to focus and apply them to Marketing Karma, as it will bring you more business, more sales, and better customers. Start by developing one killer funnel and improving it every month. Don't get distracted by new strategies or shiny objects.

Law of Focus Summary

"We cannot think of two different things simultaneously."

Marketing Karma Adaptation

Focus on your core values and primary objectives in your marketing efforts. Avoid distractions and stay true to your brand mission.

Introduction

The Law of Focus teaches that concentrating on one thing yields the best results. Maintaining a clear focus on your core values, mission, and objectives is crucial in marketing and business. For small business owners, this principle emphasizes avoiding distractions and staying true to your brand's core message and goals.

Understanding the Concept

The Law of Focus is based on the idea that divided attention leads to diminished results. In marketing, trying to appeal to everyone or pursuing too many goals can dilute your brand and confuse your audience. By focusing on what truly matters—your core values and primary objectives—you can create a robust and consistent brand that resonates with your target audience.

Applying the Law to Your Business

1. **Defining Core Values and Mission:**

   o **Mission Statement:** Develop a clear mission statement articulating your business's purpose and core values. This statement should guide all your marketing and business decisions. For example, a local organic grocery store might have a mission statement to provide the community with healthy, sustainable food options.

   o **Core Values:** Identify and clearly define your business's core values. These values should be evident in your branding, customer interactions, and business practices. A small tech startup might prioritize innovation, customer satisfaction, and sustainability.

2. **Setting Clear Objectives:**

- SMART Goals: Set Specific, Measurable, Achievable, Relevant, and Time-bound (SMART) goals for your marketing efforts. These goals provide clear direction and help maintain focus. For example, a boutique fashion brand might set a goal to increase online sales by 20% within six months through targeted social media campaigns.
- Prioritization: Prioritize your objectives based on their alignment with your core values and mission. Focus on the most impactful goals that will drive your business forward. A family-owned restaurant might prioritize enhancing customer loyalty through a rewards program over expanding its menu.

3. **Avoiding Distractions:**

- Strategic Planning: Create a marketing plan outlining your primary objectives and the steps needed to achieve them. Stick to this plan and avoid pursuing unrelated opportunities that could dilute your focus. A small fitness studio might focus on building its brand within the local community rather than expanding too quickly into new markets.
- Time Management: Implement effective time management practices to stay focused on your priorities. Allocate specific time blocks for different tasks and minimize distractions. For instance, a freelance graphic designer might dedicate mornings to client work and afternoons to marketing

their services.

4. **Consistency in Branding:**

   o **Unified Messaging:** Ensure all your
     marketing materials consistently reflect your
     core values and mission. This includes your
     website, social media profiles, advertising,
     and customer communications. A local
     coffee shop could use consistent messaging
     emphasizing its commitment to quality and
     community in all its promotional materials.
   o **Brand Guidelines:** Develop guidelines that
     outline your visual and verbal branding
     elements. These guidelines help maintain
     consistency across all platforms and ensure
     your brand remains focused. A small
     business consultant might create guidelines
     that specify using specific colors, fonts, and
     tone of voice in all communications.

Examples of Small Business Owners

Example 1: The Focused Artisan Bakery Linda
owns an artisan bakery that prides itself on using high-
quality, locally sourced ingredients. Her mission statement
emphasizes providing the community with delicious,
wholesome baked goods. Linda sets clear goals, such as
increasing her signature sourdough bread sales by 15% in
six months. She creates a strategic marketing plan that
includes social media promotions, local farmer's market
events, and in-store sampling. By focusing on her core
values and avoiding distractions, Linda has built a loyal

customer base that appreciates the quality and authenticity of her products.

Example 2: The Niche Fitness Trainer Mark is a fitness trainer specializing in strength training for seniors. He aims to help older adults improve their strength, mobility, and overall health. Mark sets specific goals, such as increasing his client base by 10% within a year through targeted online advertising and community workshops. He avoids the distraction of expanding into other fitness areas and maintains a consistent brand message that highlights his expertise and commitment to senior fitness. Mark's focused approach has made him a trusted resource in his community.

Key Takeaways

- **Clarity and Consistency:** Define your core values and mission clearly and ensure that all your marketing efforts reflect them consistently.
- **Focused Goals:** Set and prioritize SMART goals that align with your mission and values.
- **Avoid Distractions:** Stick to your strategic plan and manage your time effectively to focus on your primary objectives.

Exercises

1. **Develop a Mission Statement and Core Values:**
   - Write a clear mission statement articulating your business's purpose and core values.

Share this statement with your team and ensure it guides all your business decisions.

2. **Set SMART Goals:**
   - o Identify your primary marketing objectives and set SMART goals to achieve them. Outline the steps needed to reach these goals and regularly review your progress.

3. **Create a Strategic Marketing Plan:**
   - o Develop a strategic marketing plan that focuses on your primary objectives. Include detailed action plans for each goal and allocate resources accordingly. Avoid pursuing unrelated opportunities that could distract you from your primary objectives.

4. **Implement Brand Guidelines:**
   - o Create comprehensive brand guidelines that outline your visual and verbal branding elements. Ensure that all marketing materials adhere to these guidelines to maintain consistency and focus.

Conclusion

The Law of Focus emphasizes the importance of maintaining clarity and consistency in your marketing efforts. Small business owners can create a solid and cohesive brand identity by defining their core values and mission, setting clear objectives, avoiding distractions, and ensuring consistent branding. Embrace the principles of Marketing Karma by staying true to your brand's mission and values, and you will see positive results in your business growth and customer loyalty.

Recommendations for
Further Reading and Viewing

Books:

- "The One Thing: The Surprisingly Simple Truth Behind Extraordinary Results" by Gary Keller and Jay Papasan
- "Deep Work: Rules for Focused Success in a Distracted World" by Cal Newport

Documentaries:

- "The Social Dilemma" (2020) – Explores the dangerous human impact of social networking, with tech experts sounding the alarm on their creations.

Courses:

- "Time Management Fundamentals" on LinkedIn Learning
- "Essentialism: The Disciplined Pursuit of Less" on Skillshare

Series:

- "Abstract: The Art of Design" on Netflix – Focuses on the creative arts and the discipline of design, illustrating the importance of focused expertise.

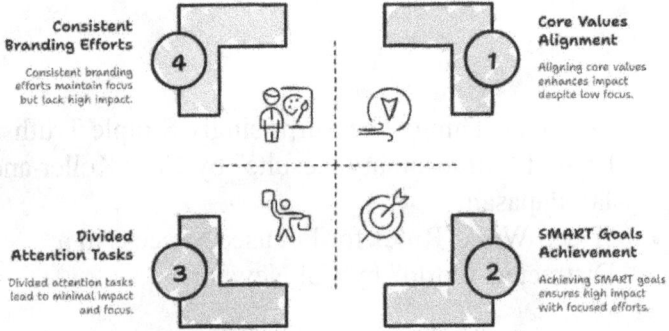

The Law of Focus in Your Business

Consistent Branding Efforts

Consistent branding efforts maintain focus but lack high impact.

4

Core Values Alignment

Aligning core values enhances impact despite low focus.

1

Divided Attention Tasks

Divided attention tasks lead to minimal impact and focus.

3

SMART Goals Achievement

Achieving SMART goals ensures high impact with focused efforts.

2

Figure 19 - The Law of Focus

Chapter 18
Law 8: The Law of Giving and Hospitality

Introduction to The Law of Giving and Hospitality

I learned about giving and hospitality from my mother and grandmother. Growing up in Tijuana, Mexico, our home was always filled with people—family, friends, and even strangers. Some stayed for a meal, others for a few days, and some for months. Many friends lived with us for years, and we often housed immigrants needing a place to stay.

When I was young, I often needed rides to school and work as I crossed the border to San Diego daily. Sometimes, I slept on friends' couches instead of returning to Tijuana. Karma works both ways. Now, I feel compelled to host as many people as possible. For twenty years, people have lived in my house.

In Marketing Karma, giving away knowledge and helping employees, suppliers, and customers is crucial. When you host webinars or speak at events, give as much information and value as possible without expecting anything in return. When an employee or colleague comes to you with a problem or seeks advice, listen, give them your time, and help without expecting anything in return.

What Exactly Is Hospitality in Marketing Karma?

After college, unable to find a job, I began teaching languages at a local school in San Diego. I had students worldwide, primarily business people, learning English or Spanish. As is customary in my family, I got to know each student personally, inviting them for coffee and showing them around San Diego and Tijuana, introducing them to great food and tequila.

One of my students, Christian Hoffman, became a good friend. We realized we shared similar views on hospitality and friendship. For an entire summer, Christian, his colleague Korina, my wife Gloria, and I enjoyed San Diego and Tijuana together. Christian invited me to work for him in Germany at the end of his stay. This single act of kindness catapulted my career and Gloria's to new heights, making us executives in our twenties. I became CEO of USA operations by the age of twenty-eight.

Christian's hospitality advanced my career and financial goals. It turned my dream of traveling through Europe from a one-month budget vacation into a year-long extravaganza with a company car. By twenty-eight, I had achieved my travel, career, and monetary goals and retired my mother and grandmother from work.

How Do You Show Giving and Hospitality?

Start by paying attention to people. In business, give value. I enjoy giving away books and samples. What will you do?

The Law of Giving and Hospitality Summary

"Our behavior should align with our beliefs."

Marketing Karma Adaptation

Practice what you preach in your marketing and business practices. Offer value and assistance to your customers without expecting immediate returns.

Introduction

The Law of Giving and Hospitality emphasizes aligning your actions with your beliefs. In business and marketing, this means offering genuine value to your customers and community without expecting immediate returns. For small business owners, this principle underscores the importance of generosity and hospitality, creating a positive impact that can lead to long-term loyalty and success.

Understanding the Concept

The Law of Giving and Hospitality is about generosity—giving without expecting anything in return. In a business context, this means providing value to your customers and community because it aligns with your values, not for immediate benefits. This approach fosters trust, goodwill, and a strong reputation, ultimately benefiting your business in the long run.

Applying the Law to Your Business

1. **Value-Driven Marketing:**

   o **Educational Content:** Create and share valuable content that educates and informs your audience. This could include blog posts, videos, webinars, or workshops. For example, a local hardware store might offer free DIY workshops and how-to videos for home improvement projects.
   o **Free Resources:** Provide free resources to help customers solve problems or achieve their goals. An accounting firm, for instance, could offer free budgeting templates or tax preparation guides on their website.

2. **Community Engagement:**

   o **Local Involvement:** Participate in community events and support local causes. This enhances your brand's reputation and strengthens your connection with the community. A small café could sponsor local art shows or participate in neighborhood clean-up events.

   o **Charitable Initiatives:** Implement philanthropic initiatives that align with your values. This could involve donating a portion of your profits to a cause, organizing fundraisers, or providing in-kind support to local organizations. A boutique clothing store might donate unsold inventory to shelters or host charity fashion shows.

3. **Customer Hospitality:**

   o **Exceptional Service:** Provide superior customer service that goes above and beyond expectations. Train your staff to be friendly, helpful, and attentive. For example, a spa could offer complimentary refreshments and personalized service to enhance the customer experience.

   o **Personal Touches:** Add personal touches to customer interactions, such as handwritten thank-you notes, personalized recommendations, or surprise gifts for loyal customers. A bookstore might send customized book recommendations based on a customer's past purchases.

Examples of Small Business Owners

Example 1: The Generous Florist

Samantha owns a small florist shop. She believes in the power of giving and often provides free floral arrangements for community events and local charities. She also offers free online tutorials on flower arranging and care tips through her social media channels. Samantha's generosity and commitment to her community have earned her a loyal customer base and a reputation for being a kind-hearted business owner.

Example 2: The Hospitable Café Owner

James runs a cozy café in a bustling neighborhood. He is dedicated to providing an exceptional customer experience and goes out of his way to make his customers feel welcome. James offers free Wi-Fi, comfortable seating, and complimentary water and snacks. He also hosts free monthly events, such as open mic nights and book clubs, to engage with the community. James's focus on hospitality has made his café a beloved local spot.

Key Takeaways

- **Align Actions with Beliefs:** Ensure your business practices reflect your core values and beliefs.
- **Offer Genuine Value:** Provide educational content, free resources, and exceptional service without expecting immediate returns.

- **Engage with the Community:** Participate in community events and support local causes to strengthen your connection with the community.

Unpacking the Law of Giving and Hospitality

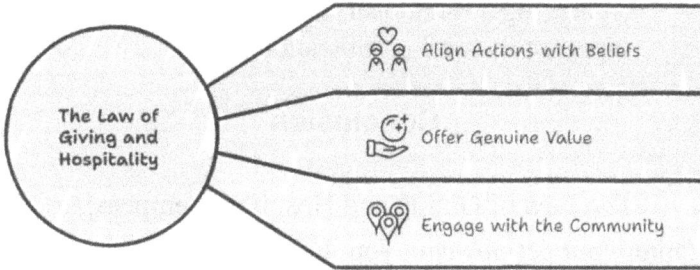

Figure 20 - The Law of Giving and Hospitality

Exercises

1. **Create Educational Content:**
   Identify topics that are valuable to your audience and create educational content around them. This could include blog posts, videos, or webinars. Share this content through your website and social media channels.
2. **Plan a Community Event:**
   Organize or participate in a community event that aligns with your values. This could be a charity fundraiser, a neighborhood clean-up, or a local festival. Use this opportunity to engage with your community and build goodwill.
3. **Enhance Customer Service:**
   Evaluate your current customer service practices

and identify areas for improvement. Train your staff
to provide exceptional service and add personal
touches to enhance the customer experience.
4. **Implement a Charitable Initiative:**
   Identify a cause that aligns with your values and
   implement a charitable initiative to support it. This
   could involve donating a portion of your profits,
   organizing a fundraiser, or providing in-kind
   support to a local organization.

Conclusion

The Law of Giving and Hospitality emphasizes
aligning your actions with your beliefs and providing
genuine value to your customers and community. By
practicing generosity and hospitality, small business
owners can create a positive impact, build trust and
goodwill, and foster long-term loyalty. Embrace the
principles of Marketing Karma by offering value without
expecting immediate returns, and you will see your
business thrive.

Chapter 19
Law 9: The Law of Here and Now

Introduction to The Law of Here and Now

One of the most essential teachings in Eastern philosophy is staying present or living in the Here and Now. It took science thousands of years to understand what this means. Even before Einstein figured out the laws of relativity and the nature of space and time, Karma understood its importance to life and happiness. Staying in the moment is not just about stopping to smell the roses; it's about experiencing something profound in every moment of our lives, not just during meditation or breaks.

To truly experience the here and now, I recommend trying two simple exercises: focused breathing and taking mental snapshots.

First Here and Now Exercise:
One Breath for Every Twelve Seconds

Let's start with breathing. The breaths you take throughout the day are automatic; we want you to notice them, at least while practicing. Start by taking a breath that lasts four seconds, hold it for four seconds, and then release it slowly for another four seconds. If four seconds is too long, try three or two seconds; if it's too easy, try five or more. Practice this throughout the day as many times as you can remember. Write it down, set an alarm, or leave a note on your desk or car. Don't worry about over breathing—feel free to do it all day. Remember to count 1, 2, 3, and 4—in, hold, and out. We focus on something simple yet good for us, which calms our nerves and muscles and centers us in the moment.

Now, let me ask you: Did you feel sad to see the seconds pass, the breaths go, or the numbers fall as you count them? Probably not. The lesson is that when you focus on the here and now, you're not suffering from past conversations, ego, or future anxieties. You're here; the numbers that come and go are unimportant. After you count 1, 2, 3, 4, you let them go, experience them, and move on to the next here and now. Congratulations, you've taken the first step toward mastering mindfulness.

For experienced meditators, try timing your slow breaths without necessarily holding them for the same number of seconds until you achieve one whole minute per breath. Once you can breathe one breath—in, hold, and out—try to inhale immediately after your final exhalation until you can take multiple breaths lasting one minute each.

Second Here and Now Exercise:
Take Mental Snapshots

The second exercise includes your surroundings, travels, family, and life. Think about where you are right now. Look around, be general, and then specific. For example, "I'm in the car listening to an audiobook on my way to work," or "I'm on vacation on an airplane reading a book." Consider your emotions: Are you content, ecstatic, or sad? Describe your environment: Is it raining or sunny? Are you in a good place or not? Take a mental snapshot of this moment with all these details—place, time, temperature, and your external and internal feelings. Think of one thing you learned today, preferably from this book. Appreciate how great it is to learn and expand your brain. Congratulations, you've taken your first snapshot, capturing a moment of self-growth, which is great for life and part of Karma.

Now for the best part: next time you're with friends or family, when you're laughing and happy, look around at their faces, feel the temperature, your surroundings, your sensations, and take a snapshot. Internally, say what you're feeling and how you're enjoying this moment. Boom, you've just taken a happy snapshot. Don't use a camera or phone; use your mind. This practice helps you stay in the moment at its best until, eventually, every moment will be the best.

I love going to concerts; a lifelong dream turned into reality. At a concert, I remember exactly where and when I first listened to that band. If I can't remember the specifics, I recall who I was with. Have you ever experienced that? It's like time travel.

I've seen many bands in Spanish and English since I grew up with both. As a Gen-X kid, I remember bands from the '80s and '90s. For example, I've seen Depeche Mode several times. I discovered them in junior high in Mexico. Listening to their songs transports me back to my friend Victor's house at twelve or thirteen, hearing those opening synthesizer chords. If you like Depeche Mode, you know what I'm talking about! I felt giddy, with a permanent grin and happy hormones flooding my brain and body. Have you felt that? Can you imagine feeling like that most of the day or your life? Wouldn't that be nice? When you listened to that song for the first time, your body registered the here and now by itself. You noticed your feelings and recorded them in a snapshot. Now, when you listen to the song, you can relive it vividly again, sometimes as if it were the first time.

With this exercise, you're experiencing the here and now and telling your brain to record it as something important, something you want to feel again. The more you practice, the more it lasts. I've been experimenting with this since I was sixteen. I also call it finding your high without actually getting high!

Marketing Karma Adaptation

Focus on the current needs and preferences of your customers. Adapt your marketing strategies to stay relevant.

Introduction

The Law of Here and Now emphasizes the importance of being present and fully engaged in the current moment. For small business owners, this principle highlights the need to focus on your customers' present needs and preferences. By staying attuned to current trends and feedback, you can adapt your marketing strategies to remain relevant and effectively meet your customers' needs.

Understanding the Concept

The Law of Here and Now is based on the idea that the present moment is where life happens. In a business context, this means focusing on current market conditions, customer preferences, and feedback to stay relevant and competitive. Ignoring the present can lead to missed opportunities and a disconnect between your business and your customers.

Applying the Law to Your Business

1. **Customer-Centric Marketing:**

   o **Listening to Feedback:** Actively seek and listen to customer feedback through surveys, social media interactions, and direct communication. For example, a small retail store might use customer surveys to gather input on product selection and shopping experience.

   o **Personalized Marketing:** Use gathered information to create customized marketing campaigns that address specific customer needs and preferences. A fitness center could tailor its promotions based on members' interests and fitness goals.

2. **Adapting to Trends:**

   o **Trend Analysis:** Stay informed about industry trends and market shifts. Use this information to adapt your product offerings and marketing strategies. For example, a bakery might introduce new flavors or products based on emerging food trends.

   o **Agility and Flexibility:** Be prepared to pivot your strategies quickly in response to changing conditions. An agile approach allows you to seize new opportunities and address challenges as they arise. A local restaurant could adjust its menu and marketing efforts based on seasonal ingredients and customer preferences.

3. **Engagement and Interaction:**

   o **Real-Time Engagement:** In real-time, engage with customers through social media, live events, and other interactive platforms. This helps build a stronger connection and keeps your brand top-of-mind. A boutique clothing store might host live fashion shows on social media to showcase new arrivals and interact with viewers.

   o **Community Building:** Foster a sense of community around your brand by creating spaces for customers to connect and share experiences. This could include online forums, social media groups, or in-person events. A tech company could create an online community where users can share tips, ask questions, and provide feedback.

Examples of Small Business Owners

Example 1: The Present-Minded Café Owner

Anna owns a café in a vibrant neighborhood. She regularly interacts with customers to understand their preferences and gathers feedback through comment cards and social media. When she noticed a growing interest in vegan options, Anna introduced a range of plant-based dishes to her menu. She also engages with her customers in real time by hosting live coffee-brewing tutorials on Instagram. By staying present and adapting to her customers' needs, Anna has built a loyal customer base and a strong community around her café.

Example 2: The Trend-Adapting Fitness Trainer
Brian is a personal trainer who stays up-to-date with the latest fitness trends and technologies. He uses social media to engage with his clients and gather feedback on their fitness goals and preferences. When he noticed a surge in interest in virtual workouts, Brian quickly adapted by offering online training sessions and creating a library of on-demand workout videos. His ability to stay present and respond to his client's needs has helped him expand his business and attract a wider audience.

Key Takeaways

- **Focus on the Present:** Stay attuned to your customer's needs and preferences.
- **Adapt to Trends:** Use trend analysis and feedback to adapt your marketing strategies and product offerings.
- **Engage in Real-Time:** Build stronger customer connections through real-time engagement and community building.

Exercises

1. **Gather Customer Feedback:**
   Implement systems to regularly gather customer feedback through surveys, social media interactions,

and direct communication. Use this feedback to identify current needs and preferences.

2. **Conduct Trend Analysis:**
   Stay informed about industry trends and market shifts. Subscribe to relevant newsletters, follow industry leaders on social media, and participate in online forums and discussions. Use this information to adapt your strategies.

3. **Plan Real-Time Engagement:**
   Develop a plan for real-time engagement with your customers. This could include live events and social media interactions.

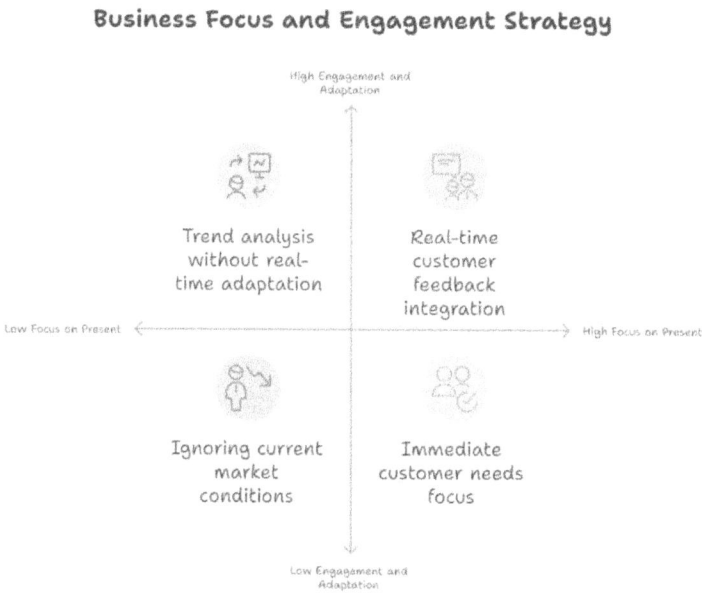

Business Focus and Engagement Strategy

High Engagement and Adaptation

Trend analysis without real-time adaptation

Real-time customer feedback integration

Low Focus on Present

High Focus on Present

Ignoring current market conditions

Immediate customer needs focus

Low Engagement and Adaptation

Figure 21 - Business Focus and Engagement Strategy

Chapter 20
Finding Your High!

With a Little Help from Your Friends

Everyone needs inspiration and motivation. The challenge is maintaining that inspiration and encouragement all the time, in every situation, with everyone. I call it "Finding Your High!"

Can you imagine being high all the time? No, not that high, the other one! Your high could be having positive thoughts, feeling content, motivated, or inspired, and feeling grand all the time, no matter what. Athletes seek that high, peak performance when playing their sport. Businesspeople strive for it, too. We should all have it in every part of our lives—as parents, children, on the job, with family and friends, while walking in the park, and when working on goals. We should all find our high.

There's a trick to finding your "Ultimate State of Happiness," or as I jokingly call it, "Your Ultimate State of Happiness." You need to break your life into phases or facets. You see, you have many facets in your life. Some depend on your age, where you were born, or what you are going through. Many rely on your goals or aspirations. We all have facets in our personality and life. We are babies, teenagers, daughters and sons, students and teachers. We are spouses, athletes, travelers, dancers, and much more. Remember, you are not just your work; you are not just what you are doing now. Those are just phases or facets. You are more than your facets.

You must find your high in every facet of your personality and every phase of your life. Don't try to find an all-encompassing global form of inspiration. Break it down!

Just as you are made of many colors, you feel differently at different times. You need other types of inspiration at varying times in your life. Sometimes, you need deep, life-changing inspiration; sometimes, you just need enough to get up from the sofa and hit the gym. Learn to see your different levels of personality, learn about yourself, what brings you inspiration, and how to find your high. Look for it in every facet of your personality and every phase of your life. Your inspiration may vary with each situation. Now, look for it.

"Your High is a Form of Inspiration that Comes from Emotional Experiences. It becomes a Source of Strength and Motivation."

Finding your high is easy if you know where to look. Now that you know you can find different sources of inspiration in various places and at other times in your life, even throughout a single day, your mission is to open your eyes. You must search for that push to reach your high for everything you want to accomplish. Find a high to better yourself, a high to help others, a high to go to the gym, a high to reconcile with a loved one, a high to be a superstar in business, and more. Open your eyes. There is inspiration in your friends, family, books, music, movies, and even people walking on the street. Inspiration is everywhere. You just have to open your eyes, look for it, be aware of it, and not let it pass you. You have to be on the lookout; otherwise, you won't see, hear, or feel it.

Don't try to find a "Comprehensive, All-Encompassing High." Your high can be one thing in one moment and change to something else at a different time. Your high should match what you are going through and what is important to you at that particular moment. Remember, your high must meet your relativity! Let me illustrate what I mean by explaining how I found my "First High."

Finding My First High

I was nine years old, living in my house in Tijuana, Mexico. I remember waking up in the middle of the night and seeing a dim light coming from my mother's room.

Curious, I got out of bed and walked toward the light. Peeking through the crack in her door, I saw my mother studying by candlelight, with three or four candles on one side and a petroleum lamp flickering on the other. She didn't see me as I watched her read and take notes. I didn't understand what she was doing or why she was up so late, but I knew it had something to do with her returning to school.

When I was very young, my mother left my father and had to work twelve hours a day to support me and send me to private school. She always emphasized the importance of education, finishing high school, and continuing college. She believed in the saying, "Do as I do, not as I say," so she decided it was necessary for her to finish high school and college. The problem was she had no time and no money. She held a full-time administrative job and attended night school; the only time left to study was at midnight. I didn't understand it then, but I did as I grew older, and I never forgot that image of her. It left a lasting impression on me.

When it was time for me to go to college, I enrolled in the USA. After all, I lived in Tijuana, the border town next to San Diego, California. Why not take advantage of that and go to school in the USA? There was a problem, though—a big one. I was a Mexican citizen living in Mexico, and non-California residents had to pay outrageously high tuition rates. I didn't have the money to spend. I also only had a tourist visa to cross the international border, and soon, my passport was revoked when border crossing agents learned of my intentions to study in the USA.

Now what? I had to turn to my father. He was an American citizen from Minnesota with an entrepreneurial spirit. He ventured to Mexico and opened several businesses, and that's how he met and married my mother. I hadn't seen my father in years, but I found him and asked him to help me acquire my American citizenship. In months, I had derived American citizenship thanks to my father and some detective work from the rest of my family, including pulling some FBI strings through my grandmother. Yes, FBI strings. My grandfather used to work for the FBI, and my grandmother cashed in that forty-year-old chip. That's another story, one of several in my book "Lessons From My Guardian Angel."

Thinking back on everything I had to overcome amazes me. I endured because I had the persistence, drive, and goodwill to change my life. It wasn't easy, and this was just the beginning. Once I started attending college in San Diego, I realized it was logistically more challenging than I had anticipated.

I commuted up to three hours to get to school and sometimes more to return home. Just getting to the border from my house was an odyssey. I had to walk about a mile, take one or two buses to the Mexico/US border, and then decide whether to cross by foot and take the trolley and bus to school (another hour) or try to hitch a ride from the cars waiting at the border. Hitching a ride was sometimes luck, sometimes skill.

I noticed that many people attending college with me lived in Tijuana and crossed the border by car every morning. I saw several vehicles with school parking permits hanging from mirrors at the border crossing. I started knocking on car windows to hitch a ride to save time and money. I was often ignored, but eventually, I got a few rides. So, I secured transportation—not the easiest way to get to school, but it worked for me.

I often didn't have money for food or the bus ride home. I used library books when I couldn't afford my own and school computers for my reports. I even spent nights at school when I couldn't get a ride or didn't have bus money to go home. I'd use the gym to shower the following day.

Throughout college, while hitching rides and sleeping on campus, I never thought my job was difficult. I never thought I had a bad deal or was dealt bad cards. After all, I had found my first high. Whenever I felt a bit sorry for myself or didn't want to get up in the morning to start my school trek, I remembered my First High. I recalled being nine years old, watching my mother studying by candlelight in the middle of the night after working all day and taking care of me. My mother finished college when I was fourteen years old. Do you think I could complain? I had it easy. I was inspired.

At 9 Years Old, I Found My First High!

When finding your high, remember it's not just one life-changing event that will forever influence your life. You can find small and different highs at different stages of your life and for various activities. Your high is a form of inspiration that comes from emotional experiences. You don't relive the experience to draw the high; you draw the power from the experience and use it to push you, calm you, wake you up, keep you going, relax, or make you feel alive.

You must find high in every situation and phase of your life. It isn't necessarily a single-encompassing high; it can be unique for every aspect and phase of your life—in sports, school, parenting, working, selling, nonprofit work, health, etc.

Your high is helpful for empowerment and inspiration and coping with stressful situations and everyday life. You're turning your experiences and the emotions produced by them into empowerment and inspiration. You need to change your thinking and philosophy towards life to achieve this. Apply the "New Theory of Relativity" from the previous chapter. See the world from your point of view and from others' points of view, and compare, adjust, and learn. This way, you can turn emotions from sorrow, anger, and helplessness into empowerment and inspiration. Let me illustrate with another example.

My New Buddy

My wife and I are blessed with wonderful lifelong friends. I could write an entire book about how each has inspired us to be better people. But now, I want to write about one friend who allowed me to find another high in my life. Despite his passing, his spirit and life inspire and motivate me daily.

I met Christian Hoffman right after college while working as a language instructor at Berlitz. He was taking English lessons, and I was intrigued by him, asking many questions about his life. I learned he was the COO of a German software company and wanted to expand the business to the United States. Before I knew it, I was on a plane to Germany to meet the owner. They initially offered me a job as a consultant, and I worked my way up to CEO of USA operations.

Christian and I worked together for several years. He was my mentor and one of my best friends. He was an imposing, tall, strong, well-mannered German who commanded attention in business meetings. He was a business powerhouse, expanding the company internationally, opening deals, and growing sales almost immediately.

I had a lot of fun working for him, but I realized some people were afraid and intimidated by him. His giant-like footsteps could be heard a mile away when he entered our office. People quickly organized their desks, fixed their ties, stood up straight, and acted busy. He had a strong presence.

Christian was a life-loving young man who was successful in business and life. I learned a lot from him, and he claimed he learned much from me. When I met him, I still lived in Mexico, and he always said that after a few years, I would impose my "Mexican ways" on his "German ways," making him a happier, warmer, more relaxed German.

Even after leaving the company, we became best friends, visited each other frequently, and spoke often. He visited us in California, and we visited him in Germany. We usually discussed culture, friendship, and life over wine. Every week, we talked about our next trip to Europe or his next trip to San Diego. His calls always put us in a good mood, as he was always upbeat, making us laugh and supporting us.

During this time, I suffered from horrible back spasms that lasted for months. I decided to call Christian to complain about my pain. A few weeks had passed, and I hadn't heard from him. I felt bad for not calling him sooner, as less important things kept me busy. When I called, he sounded tired, run-down, and lethargic. He surprised me with the terrible news that two weeks earlier, he woke up unable to move. He was paralyzed from the head down. By then, he had received treatment and could move and walk a few steps. Can you imagine how I felt about my back pain? It's all relative, remember?

Christian stayed in bed for months and preferred we not visit him. He lost a lot of weight and spent most of his last days in the hospital until he died. We were always in the dark about his illness because he couldn't explain it adequately in English. My friend died well before his time, leaving his family and friends unprepared to let him go. Christian was only 40 years old.

Christian has been physically gone for a couple of years now, but his spirit lives on in us. My wife and I frequently mention him and fondly recall our times together. Many things remind us of him, and we are learning to turn our feelings of sorrow and sadness into empowering and motivating instances.

For instance, a few months after Christian died, my wife and I were on our way to a business meeting. I had to present to a room filled with stakeholders in a new consumer product venture where I was a consultant. I didn't know anyone at the meeting, but they were supposed to be a tough, cut-throat crowd. We drove to a fancy building in downtown San Diego and rode the elevator. Before we went in, my wife asked if I was nervous. "Nervous?" I answered. "I'm a veteran of hundreds of meetings, and besides, I have an unfair advantage because I always bring Christian to my meetings, so they don't stand a chance." We walked out of the elevator, and my wife started crying, overwhelmed by emotions she couldn't control.

It's true. I always bring Christian to my meetings. I think about him every day and even speak to him sometimes. I'm sad about his death, and I can't make the sadness go away, no matter how hard I try. The one thing I can do is use my emotions and wonderful memories of him for empowerment and inspiration in my everyday life.

Chapter 21
Law 10: The Law of Change

Introduction to The Law of Change

"If nothing else, embrace change; it will keep you young."

"I hate change," I hear time and time again. Change comes in many forms. "I don't want to use AI," "I don't want to use a smartphone," "I don't want to use the internet," and "I don't want to learn to use a computer." Change applies to new music, movies, books, education, society, or life. We know that change is constant, and to stay young, our brains need to change. Without change, our brains will deteriorate.

Alright, did I scare you into change? No? Fear doesn't motivate you? Maybe this will help: If you don't feel like a new person every five years, you're not learning. Look back five years and consider everything you know now that you didn't know then. Don't focus on one thing but on everything. If your job is easy and you know everything, you're not evolving. If you don't have more social skills, you're not learning. You're stuck in an exercise plateau if you're not performing complex movements you couldn't do before. You should do difficult things to learn uncomfortable things and do them often.

Ideas for Change:

- Become a keynote speaker
- Try Yoga or Tai Chi
- Take Boxing or Martial Arts
- Shower with cold water
- Learn a new language
- Learn painting or sculpture
- Learn to be extroverted or introverted
- Learn ballroom dancing or salsa dancing
- Try Wall Climbing
- Play a new racket sport
- Teach a class; it could be on YouTube
- Study history as much as possible

If it's easy and you're already good at it, you're not changing. Change means trying something new.

Exploring Personal Growth through New Experiences

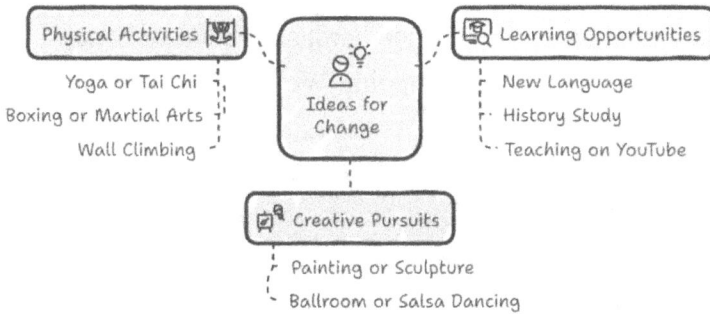

Figure 22 - Exploring Personal Growth through New Experiences

Movement Examples for Change

Tai Chi is one of the most challenging things I've done. It requires a lot of brain power. Moving in Tai Chi is like learning to walk and speak a new language simultaneously. I've practiced and taught Tai Chi for years, yet every new form makes me feel like a beginner. Holding a kick for five seconds or other balance movements is physically and mentally challenging. It's hard, and it will change your mind.

I hope many of you lift weights or do exercises involving lifting heavy things, including your body weight, like pull-ups, push-ups, muscle-ups, and handstand push-ups. It took me months to do my first muscle-up and handstand push-up, and the same with double unders and squats on a yoga ball. I started at forty-three, inviting trainers in their twenties to join me in these progressions. They tried once, found it too hard, and resumed lifting weights. They missed the point. We're not professional athletes; we're challenging our brains and bodies. If you already lift weights, seek a ridiculous goal that requires a change of mind and body.

I learned many crazy workouts from young adults training for the Olympics. They did exercises that broke my brain and body—some exercises I could never do, like jumping onto a 40-inch box while holding a medicine ball. You could also try boxing or martial arts like Kung Fu, Judo, or Brazilian Jiu-Jitsu. These will challenge both your brain and body. After a session, your core might hurt as if you did hundreds of crunches, and your mind will have had a rigorous workout as well.

Thinking Change

Some readers might find public speaking easy, while others find it terrifying. Public speaking is often feared more than death. If you think it's easy, are you any good at it? Are you sure?

Public speaking is a skill you can use every day of your life. To improve, join Toastmasters, a nonprofit that helps you become a better speaker. When I joined, I found several clubs within five miles. Toastmasters allowed me to perfect my speaking skills and learn much more. With my mentor, David Carol, I learned to mentor and train others, to motivate, give feedback, and criticize constructively. These are lessons only a few C-level executives know. You'll also learn to be quick on your feet, answering complex questions eloquently with no preparation. If public speaking isn't your thing, join a club. It will be the best thing you do all year. After a few meetings, you'll wonder how you got this far without these skills.

Learn From History

Learning history is easier said than done. What history? Which book should you read? The short answer is all of them!

No, I don't expect you to read all the history books, but you should never stop learning history. Start with what interests you, then maybe read about the places you'll visit on your next business trip or vacation. Learn about their history, culture, politics, food, music, everything. Many friends and colleagues go to Cancun without knowing it's famous for its Mayan archaeology. Take every trip, real or through a book, into history and learn from it.

Embrace anthropology, archaeology, ancient cultures and beliefs, biographies, and lessons from history, including our mistakes. Buddhism believes in reincarnation to learn lessons we didn't learn in past lives, applying those lessons until we're wise enough to enter Nirvana. Take this literally or interpret it as growing through life cycles until we have enough knowledge to become the person we were destined to be. Either way, learn from past mistakes, or you'll repeat them.

The Law of Change Summary

History Repeats Itself Until We Learn from It.

Marketing Karma Adaptation

Learn from past marketing campaigns and customer interactions. Use these insights to innovate and improve your strategies.

The Law of Change teaches that history repeats until we learn necessary lessons and make changes. In marketing and business, this principle highlights analyzing past experiences, identifying key insights, and applying these lessons to improve future strategies. Embracing change and continuously innovating is crucial for staying competitive and achieving long-term success.

Understanding the Concept

The Law of Change is based on the idea that growth comes from learning from past experiences. In business, this means analyzing previous marketing campaigns, customer interactions, and decisions to identify what worked and what didn't. By making data-driven adjustments and embracing innovation, businesses can avoid repeating past mistakes and evolve.

Applying the Law to Your Business

1. **Analyzing Past Campaigns:**

   o **Performance Metrics:** Review the performance metrics of past marketing campaigns. Identify key metrics such as engagement, conversion, and return on investment (ROI). For example, an e-commerce store might analyze email marketing campaigns to determine which generated the most sales.

   o **Customer Feedback:** Collect and analyze customer feedback from previous campaigns. This provides valuable insights into what resonated with your audience and what didn't. A local restaurant might review customer reviews and survey responses to understand their dining experience.

2. **Implementing Changes:**

- Identify Areas for Improvement: Based on your analysis, identify specific areas for improvement. Adjust your messaging, target a different audience, or change your marketing channels. For instance, a beauty salon might focus more on social media advertising after realizing it drives more engagement than print ads.
- Innovate and Experiment: Try new approaches and experiment with different strategies. This could involve launching new products, exploring new marketing platforms, or adopting new technologies. A fitness center might introduce virtual classes and online memberships to reach a wider audience.

3. **Continuous Learning:**

- Stay Informed: Keep up with industry trends and best practices by reading industry publications, attending webinars, and participating in professional networks. This helps you stay ahead of the curve and incorporate new ideas into your business. A small tech startup might subscribe to tech blogs and attend industry conferences to stay updated on the latest innovations.
- Encourage a Learning Culture: Foster a culture of continuous learning within your team. Encourage employees to pursue professional development opportunities and share their knowledge with the team. A local boutique could provide training sessions for staff on the latest fashion trends and customer service techniques.

Analyze Past
Campaigns
Reviewing previous
marketing efforts to gather
insights

Implement Data-
Driven Adjustments
Making changes based on
insights to improve
strategies

Stay Informed on
Trends
Keeping up with industry
developments and changes

Identify Key
Insights
Discovering important
lessons from past data

Innovate
Marketing
Strategies
Developing new approaches
to enhance marketing

Foster Continuous
Learning
Encouraging ongoing
education and growth within
the team

Figure 23 - The Law of Change in Business

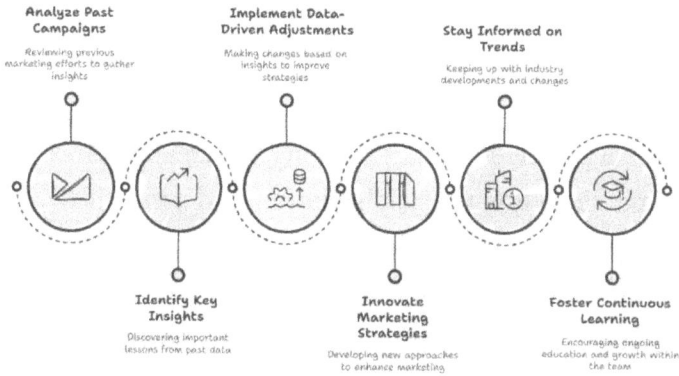

Examples of Small Business Owners

Example 1: The Adaptive Retailer

Lisa owns a small retail store that sells home decor and gifts. After analyzing her past marketing campaigns, she realized that email marketing was more effective than social media ads in driving sales. She decided to focus more on building her email list and creating personalized email campaigns. Lisa also gathered customer feedback and discovered her customers wanted more eco-friendly products. She introduced a new line of sustainable home decor items, which quickly became best-sellers. By learning from her past experiences and making strategic changes, Lisa increased her sales and customer satisfaction.

Example 2: The Innovative Fitness Trainer

Tom is a personal trainer who has been in the industry for over a decade. After noticing a decline in in-person training sessions, he analyzed his business and found many clients preferred virtual workouts. Tom pivoted his business model by offering online training sessions and creating an on-demand video library. He also introduced a monthly subscription service that provided personalized workout plans and nutrition advice. Tom's willingness to adapt and innovate allowed him to reach a broader audience and grow his business despite changing market conditions.

Key Takeaways

- **Analyze and Learn:** Regularly analyze past marketing campaigns and customer interactions to identify key insights and areas for improvement.
- **Implement Changes:** Use the insights gained to make data-driven adjustments and innovate your marketing strategies.
- **Continuous Learning:** Stay informed about industry trends and foster a culture of continuous learning within your team.

Exercises

1. **Campaign Analysis:**
   Select a recent marketing campaign and analyze its performance metrics. Identify what worked well and what didn't. Document your findings and create a plan to apply these insights to future campaigns.

2. **Customer Feedback Review:**
   Collect and review customer feedback from various sources such as surveys, reviews, and social media comments. Identify common themes and areas for improvement. Use this feedback to make necessary changes to your products, services, or marketing strategies.
3. **Innovation Plan:**
   Develop a plan to incorporate new ideas and innovations into your business. Identify one or two new approaches you want to try and outline the steps needed to implement them. Set specific goals and metrics to measure their success.
4. **Professional Development:**
   Encourage your team to pursue professional development opportunities. Identify relevant courses, webinars, or industry events that can enhance their skills and knowledge. Create a schedule for regular training sessions and knowledge-sharing meetings.

Conclusion

The Law of Change emphasizes the importance of learning from past experiences and making data-driven adjustments to improve future outcomes. By analyzing past marketing campaigns, implementing strategic changes, and fostering a culture of continuous learning, small business owners can stay competitive and achieve long-term success. Embrace the principles of Marketing Karma by being adaptable and open to change, and you will see positive results in your business growth and customer satisfaction.

Chapter 22
Your Magnetic Personality

Promote Yourself Using Magnets

No, I won't make you wear magnets. No magnetic earrings, stickers, or shoes. You won't need to create magnet business cards or calendars for clients to attach to their refrigerators—unless you want to. Instead, you'll use the Promotional Tool of Magnets to attract the right people, attract attention, and create opportunities for yourself.

Reader Beware: Magnets can also attract the wrong kind of attention, people, or reactions. This is the trick with magnets; they have two sides. Let's learn "Magnet Management." Magnet Management is about how to turn the attraction side of your magnet and keep the rejection side under control.

You might be asking, "What does Jorge mean by magnets?" Magnets have the power to both attract and repel. In your "promotion toolbox," you have many types of magnets. You probably use some of them already, but not all of them. You need to recognize and know what they are and how they can be used "for good or evil."

Magnetic Personality: Is It a Good Thing?

We've all heard the expression "magnetic personality." We assume it's a good thing that these people attract others to them. Now, we will explore the Magnetic Personality Myth to see how we can use it for self-promotion and, more importantly, how to avoid using it negatively.

Earlier in the book, I mentioned you'll have not just a gravitational pull, not just a magnetic personality, but an electromagnetic force. This means you'll be as powerful as the forces binding atoms and molecules. That's strong!

Having a magnetic personality means you're using certain tools from your Promotional Toolbox to attract or repel people. You might think you don't have control over your magnetism, that it's a personality trait some people have and others don't. Actually, it's not. Many of your magnets can be turned on and off. They can be used at different times and in different circumstances to either attract or repel people. Do you want to attract people more often with a positive magnetic personality? It's easy. Just change your magnets—use the positive ones and avoid the negative ones. People will start being attracted to you.

If you're always smiling, happy, making people laugh, and making others feel comfortable, people will want to be around you. You don't have to be the center of

239

attention; you just have to be happy and try to make others happy. Listen to others before you speak, engage with people in a positive tone, and be comprehensive and caring. This will start turning you into a lean, mean, magnetic machine!

Avoiding Negative Magnets

We often show our negative side, our bad magnets, unconsciously when we are annoyed, in a bad mood, depressed, or when things don't go our way. We might try to hide our bad magnets and only use them at home or with our family. But that doesn't work; our family is the center of our magnetism, the center of our Karma. If you don't completely attract your family members or your immediate circle, you won't be able to go beyond that circle and attract others. Think of that before you snap at your spouse or use an exasperated tone with your kids.

I've seen marriages end, friendships deteriorate, and family relationships suffer because people choose negative magnets over positive ones. I've heard people say, "This is how I am. I can't change who I am. Take me or leave me." More often than not, people will leave you. Most people want to be around positive and joyful individuals.

Consistency in Your Magnetism

Think of your magnetism as the force of gravity in the solar system. You are the sun—bright, big, and with tremendous forces of attraction. The sun can't turn off its gravity and then turn it back on; the planets would fly away, never to return. Apply this Karma Tool to your life and your self-promotion. Don't change from attracting to repelling, from negative to positive. When you are constantly negative, criticizing others, and snapping, you can't just make it better by turning on the charm occasionally. One day, the planets will fly away, and you will be a lonely sun in the universe with nothing to attract.

Imagine you're hosting a party, and more people show up than expected. You might not have enough food, drinks, or chairs. Your spouse and other family members forgot to tell you they invited more guests. You're frustrated, maybe getting angry. What do you do? Where are your magnets? Will you snap at your spouse to show your anger? Probably. But that's the point of having a magnetic personality—you have complete control over it. You can choose to snap, get frustrated, and worry, or you can choose to be happy. Remember, you are lucky—lucky enough to have a house full of people and to host a party. So feel lucky and continue using your positive magnets.

Be Tougher on Yourself to Be Better with Others

We face many situations throughout our day, week, and life that force us to react. We don't always have time to stop, think, and develop sentiments towards someone or something. We just react quickly. This reaction seems like a split-second decision, but it's really a reflection of our Karma. You might say, "That's just my personality." You're right. Now, what are you going to do about it?

Before you change your magnets, you need to pay attention to them. This is called consciousness. Consciousness isn't just about concentration or lack of concentration. It's not just about where you left your keys or the time and place you're living. That's the first step of consciousness—being aware of our surroundings and how we fit into that world. This is space and time. For example, you're reading or listening to this book right now, aware of where you are, maybe sitting in a chair or on a couch. You're aware that it is "right now," feeling time pass even if you stay in the same place. If you lift your eyes from the book, you'll see what's around you. This is part of your consciousness. If you don't see it or notice it, it's not part of your consciousness.

The second part of your consciousness is turning your eyes inside out. When you look inside and notice what you're doing, feeling, thinking, and saying, this alone will stop the negative magnets from activating. The ability to self-analyze and reach higher consciousness is not new. Like Karma, it comes from Hinduism and has influenced other beliefs and religions like Buddhism, Zen, and even Taoism in China. The meditative and introspective practices of the third eye are seen in most mainstream religions.

Using the Third Eye

The third eye, a gate located between your eyebrows, according to Hinduism, sees more than just space and time. It sees inside you and takes you to higher planes of consciousness. In Marketing Karma, we'll use our third eye to observe not only situations but also feelings. Yes, feelings. If you imagine, you can see feelings, and you can bring them to the realm of reality. You can touch them, control them, and dismantle them to throw them in the trash. We're targeting your bad feelings, especially anger— a primitive feeling that helped us in pre-historic times but now only gets us into trouble.

From now on, pay attention to your feelings—all of them, all the time. When you're happy, think about how happiness feels. For me, it feels like a warm ray of sunlight in my body—warm, bright, and paralyzing. Think of bottling that feeling and drinking it when you need it. Do the same with anger. Follow it around, get to know it, and feel it in your skin. How does it feel? Is it cold? Scorching? Does it go to your stomach before bubbling up and escaping through your mouth with a snappy remark? Get to know your anger and other negative feelings. After a few weeks, you'll see them coming. They will be predictable. And as you know, what's predictable is avoidable. The next time a bad magnet starts to surface, you'll easily wave it away. You'll stay quiet or take an insult and laugh. Two minutes later, you'll bask in your sun of happiness.

Once you use your positive magnets constantly and consciously, you won't react negatively in tough situations. You won't tolerate that from yourself. You will start seeing a shift in how you perceive the same situations and actually get angry with yourself if you react badly or make someone feel uncomfortable. You will be tougher on yourself to be better with others.

Now that you know the different types of magnetic personalities, those that attract and those that repel, think about your magnets throughout the day. When you're walking, talking, or interacting with others, when you are alone in your car or at home—think about what you do to attract people, your family, your friends, colleagues, even strangers. Think about what you do to push them away, and compensate, learn, and apply the tools of attraction.

Let's review some of these specific tools and how to use them.

Magnets for Life: Marketing Karma

Positive Magnets:

- Smile
- Compliment
- Listen
- Politeness
- Helpfulness
- Sympathy
- Tolerance
- Charity/Humanity
- Good Tone of Voice
- Positive Body Language
- Acceptance

Negative Magnets:

- Snap
- Roll Eyes
- Make Negative Sounds
- Criticize
- Interrupt
- Disrespect
- Stone Wall
- Gossip

Which marketing approach should be adopted?

Positive Magnets

These actions foster a positive marketing environment and build strong relationships.

Negative Magnets

These actions can harm relationships and create a negative marketing impact.

Figure 24 - Magnets for Life

Chapter 23
Law 11: The Law of Patience and Reward

"God, I Want Patience,
and I Want It Right Now!"

Remember the breathing exercise? The simple one: four seconds in, four seconds hold, and four seconds out? Are you still doing it? It requires patience!

Every aspect of Karma requires patience—from being present to focusing on one task or one marketing funnel at a time. Patience is not just a philosophical concept; it is practical. It's waiting for someone to finish their sentence without interrupting, learning a new skill, and mastering a new art.

Patience is attempting your first pull-up, even if it takes a year. It's writing a four-hundred-page book, one letter at a time. It's letting your kids learn a lesson on their own without giving them the answer right away. Life requires patience.

When I run a marketing campaign, I test as much as possible. I might test articles on LinkedIn, TikTok videos, and Meta headlines. Each piece of information gets tested individually. Once I find the winner, I test it in combination and then against proprietary AI to predict better outcomes. Yes, I use AI daily, and my team does too. Given this, do you give up on a funnel after some keyword research? Or when an ad doesn't sell immediately? That's the opposite of this law—that's impatience, the antagonist. You don't want to be the villain in your marketing story. Use the laws of Marketing Karma and have patience. Follow each step meticulously; don't skip any. This process requires patience.

In my first couple of jobs after college in the software industry, my patience was challenged by long sales cycles. It took anywhere from three to sixteen months to sell the software. At twenty-six, a year seemed like a lifetime. When my partner Sandro and I wanted to work with Snoop Dogg, it took us a year to attract him and his team, six months to finish branding and prototyping, and another six months for the products to start selling. When Sandro and I wanted to go public for the second time, it took us four tries to succeed.

In real life, you might be recovering from an addiction, mourning, or an accident—have patience. In the world of marketing, personal growth combined with patience is the stuff of legends.

The Law of Patience and Reward Summary

*"Rewards Come from Persistent and
Patient Work."*

Marketing Karma Adaptation

Consistent and patient marketing efforts yield long-term success. Focus on building relationships rather than quick wins. Test meticulously to find your perfect consumer, even if it takes forever.

Introduction to The Law of Patience

The Law of Patience and Reward teaches that lasting rewards come from persistent and patient efforts. In marketing and business, this principle highlights the importance of consistent, long-term strategies over short-term gains. For small business owners, embracing patience and persistence in marketing efforts can lead to sustainable growth, stronger customer relationships, and increased loyalty.

Understanding the Concept

The Law of Patience and Reward is based on the idea that true success comes from steady, persistent effort over time. In marketing, this means that building a strong brand and loyal customer base requires ongoing commitment and consistency. Quick wins may provide temporary boosts, but sustainable success is achieved through long-term strategies and relationship-building. Marketing takes patience—even with a master's in marketing, you still need to test. The real answers come from testing, honing the perfect mix of headline, media, delivery, and audience selection. Every comma of this sentence takes patience.

Applying the Law to Your Business

1. **Consistent Marketing Efforts:**

    o **Regular Content Creation:** Develop a content calendar and commit to regularly creating and sharing valuable content. This could include blog posts, social media updates, videos, and newsletters. For example, a local bakery might share weekly recipes, baking tips, and behind-the-scenes looks at their kitchen.

    o **Steady Social Media Presence:** Maintain a consistent presence on social media platforms. Post regularly, engage with your audience, and respond to comments and messages promptly. A boutique clothing store might post daily outfit inspirations and customer spotlights on Instagram.

2. **Relationship Building:**

- **Customer Engagement:** Focus on building genuine relationships with your customers. Engage with them through personalized communication, loyalty programs, and exceptional customer service. A small café could implement a loyalty card program and send personalized thank-you notes to regular customers.
- **Community Involvement:** Participate in local events and support community initiatives. This helps build a positive reputation and fosters a sense of loyalty among local customers. A fitness studio might sponsor local sports events or host free community workout sessions.

3. **Long-Term Strategies:**

- **Brand Building:** Invest in building a strong, recognizable brand over time. This includes maintaining a consistent brand voice, visual identity, and messaging. A craft brewery might focus on creating a unique brand story and consistently using it across all marketing materials.
- **Customer Retention:** Develop strategies to retain existing customers and encourage repeat business. This could involve personalized follow-ups, special offers for loyal customers, and ongoing engagement. A hair salon might offer discounted rates for regular clients or a referral bonus program.

Examples of Small Business Owners

Example 1: The Persistent Boutique Owner

Emily owns a boutique that sells handmade jewelry. She understands the importance of patience and consistency in marketing. Emily creates a content calendar and posts regularly on her blog and social media channels, sharing jewelry-making tutorials, styling tips, and customer testimonials. She engages with her followers by responding to comments and messages. Over time, Emily has built a loyal customer base that appreciates her consistent efforts and the value she provides.

Example 2: The Engaging Café Owner

John runs a cozy café in a small town. He believes in building strong relationships with his customers and being an active part of the community. John participates in local events, supports community initiatives, and offers a loyalty program to reward regular customers. He maintains a consistent presence on social media, sharing daily specials, customer stories, and community news. John's patient and persistent efforts have made his café a beloved spot in the community.

Key Takeaways

- **Consistency is Crucial:** Maintain consistent marketing efforts to build a strong, recognizable brand and loyal customer base.

- **Focus on Relationships:** Prioritize building genuine relationships with your customers through personalized engagement and community involvement.
- **Long-Term Success:** Embrace long-term strategies over short-term gains to achieve sustainable growth and customer loyalty.

Building Sustainable Marketing Success

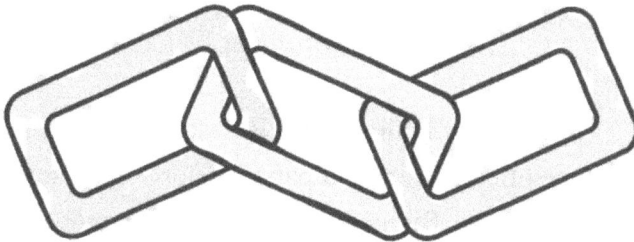

Consistency

Maintaining steady efforts for brand recognition

Relationship Focus

Engaging with customers personally and community-wise

Long-Term Strategies

Prioritizing long-term gains over short-term wins

Figure 25 - The Law of Patience and Reward

Exercises

1. **Create a Content Calendar:**
   Develop a content calendar for your business. Plan and schedule regular content updates, such as blog

posts, social media updates, and newsletters. Stick to this schedule to maintain consistency.

2. **Implement a Loyalty Program:**
   Design and implement a loyalty program to reward regular customers. This could include a points-based system, special discounts, or exclusive offers for loyal customers.

3. **Engage with Your Community:**
   Identify local events and community initiatives that align with your values and participate in them. This could involve sponsoring events, hosting workshops, or supporting local charities.

4. **Track Customer Engagement:**
   Monitor your customer engagement efforts by tracking metrics such as social media interactions, email open rates, and customer feedback. Use this data to refine your strategies and improve customer relationships.

Conclusion

The Law of Patience and Reward emphasizes the importance of consistent and patient efforts in achieving long-term success. By maintaining consistent marketing efforts, building genuine relationships with customers, and focusing on long-term strategies, small business owners can create a strong, loyal customer base and sustainable growth. Embrace the principles of Marketing Karma by practicing patience and persistence, and you will see the rewards in your business success.

Chapter 24
Law 12: The Law of Significance and Inspiration

Introduction to
The Law of Significance and Inspiration

In marketing, you need a USP and UVP—a Unique Selling Proposition and a Unique Value Proposition. Your UVP embodies your beliefs, the values you hold for yourself, your family, your company, and what you want to contribute to your employees, suppliers, and customers. Your USP is how you communicate these values to the market. When you spread these values, you inspire and add value to the world. That's the significance of your actions, your values, and your marketing. This is why I wrote this book—to share something with you, to inspire you, and in your inspiration, to find my own meaning in the world. This is why I love writing; it might be the way I leave a lasting mark. How about you? What's your significance? What do you wish to inspire?

Are you feeling passionate? If you find great products and services to sell, you should feel passionate. If not, maybe you need to find something special, including yourself, and sell that. Your passion shows through your actions, and you'll achieve more if you believe in your products and yourself.

When my friend Alejandro Jimenez approached me about creating programs for entrepreneurs in Spanish, I immediately said yes. We knew we could make a difference in the lives of new entrepreneurs, especially in the USA and Mexico. Growing up, Alejandro and I had no access to entrepreneurship or business training in Mexico. Now, we want to provide this information to anyone— through books, lectures in businesses, organizations, and schools, videos, courses, and all forms of communication.

When I wrote my first book, *Build Your Beverage Empire*, it was out of frustration with the lack of resources for starting a beverage company. Later, I wrote *"Wholesale MBA"* to share my knowledge of consumer goods sales and marketing. Before writing those books, I spent hundreds of hours giving free teleseminars and later webinars. I wanted to bridge the gap between an idea and the knowledge to execute it. I discovered that beverage entrepreneurs often spent two years and two hundred thousand dollars developing a beverage that could be developed in three months and ten thousand dollars. I wanted to give value, to inspire, and to find meaning. What I received in return was Karma. Those books catapulted my entrepreneurial life to where I am now.

The Law of Significance and Inspiration Summary

"Our Contributions Have Value and Impact."

Marketing Karma Adaptation

Your marketing efforts should inspire and add value to your audience. Create meaningful content that resonates with your customers.

Introduction to The Law of Significance and Inspiration

The Law of Significance and Inspiration emphasizes that every action we take and every contribution we make has value and impact. In marketing and business, this principle highlights the importance of creating meaningful and inspiring content that adds value to your audience. For small business owners, focusing on significant contributions can lead to deeper customer connections, stronger brand loyalty, and a positive reputation.

Understanding the Concept

The Law of Significance and Inspiration is based on the idea that our actions and contributions can make a difference. In marketing, this means that the content and messages we share should not only promote our products or services but also inspire and add value to our audience. By creating meaningful and impactful content, businesses can build stronger relationships with their customers and foster a sense of loyalty and trust.

Applying the Law to Your Business

1. **Meaningful Content Creation:**

   o **Value-Driven Content:** Create content that provides genuine value to your audience. This could include educational resources, inspirational stories, and practical tips. For example, a small garden center might create blog posts and videos on gardening techniques, plant care, and landscaping ideas.

   o **Storytelling:** Use storytelling to connect with your audience on an emotional level. Share stories that highlight your brand values, customer experiences, and community involvement. A local bakery could share the stories behind their recipes, the farmers they source ingredients from, and the community events they support.

2. **Inspiration Through Leadership:**

- Lead by Example: Demonstrate your commitment to your values and mission through your actions. This could involve sustainable business practices, ethical sourcing, and community involvement. A boutique clothing store might highlight its use of eco-friendly materials and fair trade practices.
- Encourage and Empower: Inspire your customers and community by encouraging and empowering them to take positive action. This could involve hosting workshops, providing resources, and creating opportunities for collaboration. A fitness studio could offer free wellness workshops and encourage members to share their fitness journeys.

3. **Engaging and Interactive Content:**

- Interactive Campaigns: Create campaigns that engage your audience and encourage participation. This could include contests, challenges, and user-generated content. A local bookstore might host a reading challenge where customers share their progress and reviews on social media.
- Community Building: Foster a sense of community by creating spaces for your customers to connect and interact. This could involve online forums, social media groups, or in-person events. A tech company could create an online community where users share tips, ask questions, and collaborate on projects.

Examples of Small Business Owners

Example 1: The Inspirational Artisan

Sophie runs a small artisan soap business. She believes in the power of natural ingredients and sustainable practices. Sophie creates blog posts and videos that educate her customers about the benefits of natural skincare and the importance of sustainability. She shares stories about the local farmers who supply her ingredients and the environmental initiatives she supports. Sophie's commitment to meaningful content and ethical practices has inspired a loyal customer base that values her products and mission.

Example 2: The Community-Focused Coffee Shop

Ben owns a coffee shop in a busy neighborhood. He is dedicated to creating a welcoming and inspiring space for his community. Ben hosts free events such as poetry readings, live music, and art exhibitions, providing a platform for local artists and performers. He also shares stories about his team, the coffee growers he partners with, and the community projects he supports. Ben's focus on creating meaningful and inspiring content has made his coffee shop a beloved community hub.

Key Takeaways

- **Create Value-Driven Content:** Focus on creating content that provides genuine value and inspiration to your audience.
- **Lead by Example:** Demonstrate your commitment to your values and mission through your actions and leadership.
- **Engage and Inspire:** Foster engagement and community by creating interactive and meaningful content that resonates with your customers.

Exercises

1. **Content Planning:**
   Develop a content plan that focuses on providing value and inspiration to your audience. Identify key topics and themes that align with your brand values and mission. Create a schedule for producing and sharing this content.
2. **Storytelling:**
   Identify stories that highlight your brand values, customer experiences, and community involvement. Share these stories through various channels, such as your website, social media, and newsletters.
3. **Interactive Campaigns:**
   Plan and execute an interactive marketing campaign that encourages audience participation. This could include contests, challenges, or user-generated content initiatives. Monitor engagement and gather feedback to refine future campaigns.
4. **Community Engagement:**
   Create opportunities for your customers to connect and interact. This could involve online forums, social media groups, or in-person events. Foster a

sense of community and encourage collaboration and sharing.

Conclusion

The Law of Significance and Inspiration emphasizes the importance of creating meaningful and impactful content that adds value to your audience. By focusing on value-driven content, leading by example, and fostering engagement and community, small business owners can build deeper connections with their customers and create a positive and inspiring brand presence. Embrace the principles of Marketing Karma by making significant contributions through your marketing efforts, and you will see a positive impact on your business growth and customer loyalty.

The Law of Significance and Inspiration

Create Value-Driven Content

Focus on content that provides genuine value and inspiration to the audience.

Lead by Example

Demonstrate commitment to values and mission through actions and leadership.

Engage and Inspire

Foster engagement and community with interactive and meaningful content.

Figure 26 - The Law of Significance and Inspiration

Chapter 25
Be a Dream Maker

Bring Them with You

It's easy to win when it's just you. I'm not talking about individual sports like tennis, bowling, or running. I mean controlling and influencing the many aspects of our lives—our successes, failures, relationships, future, and even our health. Most importantly, we can control our happiness. You can decide to be "Happy, Healthy, and Wealthy." This is straightforward; it's like playing golf. It's all on you!

By now, you should grasp Marketing Karma and understand that you can control it. Later, you'll learn how to apply it in everyday life. By the middle of this book, you'll have sophisticated tools to promote yourself to the world. But with great power comes great responsibility. After finishing this book, you'll harness and use these powers for good.

So, no more playing golf with your newfound powers. You're into team sports now! You not only have to win but also help others win. You need to help others be Happy, Healthy, and Wealthy—not just yourself. Start with yourself, then move to your immediate circle: your spouse, kids, parents, siblings, and co-workers. Expand your reach to friends, extended family, your community, and eventually, the world!

Always expect to win! In life, business, family, health, wealth, and friendships—expect it. You control it. The challenge is bringing others along. Help others achieve happiness, health, and wealth. Then you'll not only be a winner; you'll be a champion.

Help Others Be Happy, Healthy, and Wealthy. Then You'll Be Not Just a Winner, You'll Be a Champion.

Winning is easy. If you don't agree now, you will after discovering the meaning and methodology of Marketing Karma. If it's easy to win, why stop there? Why not persist and make winners of others? It will bring happiness to others and satisfaction to you.

This is why this book emphasizes "Unselfish" in the title. Imagine gaining all this power without any responsibility. That wouldn't be very responsible, would it?

Besides, once you are completely happy, healthy, and wealthy, what? Will you retire from Marketing Karma? Turn it off? Go live alone in the wilderness? No, that's not realistic. You must live with others, socialize, and bring people with you on the journey of unselfish promotion. They'll enjoy life, help others, and be Happy, Healthy, and Wealthy in your company. Or do you want to be alone at the top, alone at the finish line, alone on your yacht?

Alone on Your Yacht

Let's say you're a business person or investor. You've made it big and have the toys to prove it—fast cars, mansions, even a huge luxury yacht. Picture yourself in the yacht's Jacuzzi, sipping your favorite drink in the middle of the ocean, enjoying the sun and fresh air—alone.

Everything sounded great until the "alone" part, right? That's the point. It's easy to be on "Your High," but can you share that high with your friends? Can you bring them with you? Do you want them there, enjoying the company and the yacht, or would you rather be alone?

Dear Dream Maker

It's easy to have dreams; it's harder to make them come true. Making dreams come true for others is even harder. I'm not talking about giving away Ferraris. I mean giving opportunities—jobs, houses, cars, a better standard of living—to others, whether they're part of your circle of friends, family, or even strangers. And yes, there is something in it for you.

When you put other people first, they will do the same for you. It's simple but true. Do the math. If you prioritize the interests of five people, they will put you at the top of their lists. That's five lists! This will pay off. How do you put others' interests ahead of yours? Start with your immediate circle—family, friends, and co-workers. Practice with them, then broaden your reach.

Being a Dream Maker makes you an instant Marketing Karma expert. Your phone will ring, your email inbox will fill up, and people will seek your help, advice, and business.

Chapter 26
Always Be Selling

You Are Always On!

When I struggled to choose my major in college, I never thought, "I'm going to be in sales when I graduate." It was the furthest thing from my mind. I never wanted to sell anything, nor did I intend to be a salesperson. I always pictured a used car salesperson hounding and pushing people to make a sale. I told myself, "I'm not doing that."

Gradually, I realized that many social interactions, not just commercial ones, involve sales. Whether in normal conversations, social gatherings, convincing your kids or spouse to do something or many other social activities, you're often persuading others or getting your point across. Viewing it this way started to change my mind about selling. I saw that we are always selling. When making a point, we use sales skills. As children, when we want a toy, we convince our parents using tools from begging to crying to logic. As students, if we need a grade changed, we sell our point to the teacher. To get into a full class, we sell ourselves. In many daily situations, we're always selling.

Later, in the workplace and in my "grown-up life," I discovered that everything is related to selling. Writing a resume is crafting a sales letter; an interview is a sales meeting; getting a raise is an up-sell; getting a promotion is a long sales cycle. And this applies to any job, not just sales jobs. I was surprised. I thought I would never have to sell anything.

I started studying sales and applying sales techniques to various life events, especially my job. For example, when I discovered that getting a raise was just an up-sell and that closing a deal could take multiple sales calls, I started asking for a raise every couple of months. If I got a "no," I asked again and again, changing my strategy each time. When I finally got a raise, I asked for another in three months. Then I asked for a promotion. If I got a "no," I asked what I needed to do to get the promotion, did it, and asked again. This was my first job out of college, and I didn't know any better. The result was my first CEO position at age twenty-eight for an ERP software company. I thought to myself, ABS—Always Be Selling!

As a teenager, I equated selling with influence. Whether in family, politics, religion, or anything requiring action, influence was key. If I wanted to help a friend stop using drugs, I used influence. To get my mother's permission to spend the night at a friend's house, I had to use influence. As I grew up, I discovered that mastering influence requires marketing and sales skills.

As a business mentor, martial arts instructor, keynote speaker, and business owner, I use influence all the time. In business, with employees, clients, and prospects. As a mentor to my clients. As a martial arts instructor, especially with children. With family, I try to steer the younger generations to follow their dreams, be happy, and stay on the right path. Yes, it's all influence.

See selling as a new kind of word. It's not a bad word; it's actually a good one. Sales strategies are based on observation, listening, making people happy, and solving problems. These four points form a solid base for unselfish self-promotion. You can't go wrong in self-promotion when you're making people happy and solving their problems, which is what selling is all about. A good salesperson achieves these two goals. So be a good salesperson and start making more people happy and solving more problems.

Five Basic Points When Selling:

1. Observation
2. Listening
3. Making others happy
4. Solving problems
5. Storytelling

ABS (Always Be Selling) means you are always at your best. You are always smiling, always watching out for other people's needs and wants. You behave well, avoid foul language, maintain your image, and act as your best brand manager.

Remember, you are always selling; you are always on. I've noticed how restaurant waiters behave on and off the floor. For waiters, the kitchen is next to the restaurant floor, and the stations are on the floor. In high-end, expensive restaurants where they can make great tips, waiters are usually very professional, friendly, and well-behaved. But when they go to their station, the kitchen, or behind the counter with other employees, listen closely. You will often hear foul language, loud conversations, counting tips, or making loud jokes about customers. Observe them next time you're in a restaurant. Not to criticize but to learn what it takes to always be on to ABS.

Discovering Sales

I didn't know that we were always selling. Like many of this book's points, tools, and strategies, I discovered it through my life experiences. Even though I now see every job or business as a "sales position," I didn't always see it this way. I never wanted to sell anything. One day, at about twenty years old, a friend asked me to work at a men's clothing retail store as a clerk during the Christmas season. I needed the money and couldn't get any of the jobs I wanted, so I took it. It turns out that being a clerk in a retail store means you are a salesperson. Oh no!

There I was, a new kid among old pros. My colleagues were all professional retail salespeople, some with twenty years of experience. I watched how they worked, how they interacted with customers, how they approached them, and how they sold. I didn't like it. Yes, they were well-trained and experienced and sold very well, but I didn't like their methods. The other salespeople weren't selling themselves; they weren't solving a problem or fulfilling a want; they were just selling.

After a while, I decided to place myself in the customer's shoes. When I go into a store, I don't like people following me around or standing behind me. I don't like it when they ask if they can help me. So, I ignored my retail sales training and my colleagues' coaching, and I followed my gut—my Marketing Karma gut feeling. When customers came in, I still approached them as required by company policy but not to sell them anything. I provided information. I told them where the deals were when we would have discounts, what to avoid, and if another store had specials. My boss didn't like my approach. She said I was not selling; I was sending people to the back of the store to buy from the discount rack or to other stores. I told her I would love it if someone did that for me when shopping.

Imagine walking into a store, and the salesperson tells you the truth: that their clothes are overpriced, you can find something cheaper down the street, the best deals are in the back, and the items in the front will be marked down next week. Wow, I would love that. Unfortunately, no one has ever helped me like that. I decided to be the first! I put myself in the customers' shoes. I looked out for them, helping them understand who they are, why they are shopping, and their budget. I spent most of my time asking questions and listening to customers. My boss thought these were all my friends visiting because I spent so much time conversing with them. They were customers.

The result? I was number one in sales in nine out of ten categories, outselling the old pros. The one category I didn't win was items sold per transaction. When someone bought one item, I didn't up-sell them if they didn't need it. I lost that category.

This is when I discovered selling wasn't so bad. I never thought I was selling. I ignored my sales goals and just focused on making people happy and solving their problems. In the process, I made friends and had a good time. I didn't make much money in that job; I was making minimum wage with no commissions. But the knowledge I gained was invaluable. Aside from making great friends and having terrific experiences, I discovered the principles of ABS—Always Be Selling. When you work in retail, you must be happy, smiling, charming, looking great, well-groomed, and on your best behavior. You always have to be on, always be selling. This isn't just selling; it's

Marketing Karma: making others happy and being number one in sales.

This example isn't just for a sales position; it's not aimed solely at making you a better retail salesperson. It's making a point: the traditional meaning of "sales" doesn't apply in Marketing Karma. The new meaning of sales is that you are always on. You are at your best; you are solving problems and representing yourself in the best way possible. You must pass through all socioeconomic barriers—first impression, second impression, and third impression—to get to the real you. We will cover more about first impressions and how people see you when we discuss advanced strategies and your image. For now, be on your best behavior, look your best, feel like a million bucks, make people happy, solve their problems, and Always Be Selling.

Selling Is a Science, Not an Art

"You can't teach others how to sell." This is a theory I hear time and time again. "You must be born a salesperson; you can't teach it." "Either you have it or you don't." "Selling is an art." Well, nonsense. Selling is a science. You can experiment with it, apply the same rules, and produce the same results. There isn't ONE style of sales; there isn't ONE type of salesperson or personality. You don't have to be fast-talking, extroverted, or "smooth."

Salespeople can be pretty introverted and even rough around the edges.

Everyone is a salesperson. You might think you aren't a salesperson, and you might be right. Most likely, you are wrong (sorry). You probably sell almost every day of your life without knowing it. You have sold if you have asked for a job or been in a job interview, asked someone on a date, convinced your kids to do something, convinced your parents you needed to do something, asked for a raise, or asked for a discount on a car or other purchase. Many decisions in life are sales decisions. In many of these, you either sell or are sold to. If you didn't get a raise, your boss sold you. If your kids didn't do what you wanted, they sold you. If you got that discount you wanted on a car, you sold them. Well, now that we've established that everyone is a salesperson and that you face one sales situation after another, don't you think you should at least know a bit about selling? How do you get that job, that discount, convince your kids, or even your spouse?

You are always on. Remember, you are always on, always working, selling, promoting, helping. When you are out, at parties, traveling, always be on. Always look at your image, have business cards, behave, and be on.

Always be needy! Why do I say this? Always be needy. Awaken your mind's caveman survival mode, and always keep it on. This is the NEED to survive. Survive when you need to climb a mountain, run away from a tiger, or when you lose your job. Always be needy, always be on!

Practical Sales Tips and Techniques

Storytelling is my favorite way of selling. It's the oldest oral tradition that we know about, and humans have over two hundred and fifty thousand years of practice in learning from stories. Stories are the foundation of our religions and constitutions, and they're the way we remember important things.

When I was twenty years old, I decided memory was one of the most important things in my growth. So, I took memory courses and diligently practiced daily for two years until I could memorize one hundred words. Upon completion of my memory studies, I could vividly remember my past and grasp important subjects that I could apply immediately in business and my personal life. Most of my memory training was based on storytelling; why? Because we are programmed to remember stories. So, when the memory training asked me to commit words to memory, the technique was to waive a fantastic story with the words; it works like a charm!

Embrace storytelling, become a storyteller, practice it, write stories, and create memories with your stories. My books are my number one marketing tool, and they are filled with stories; however, you don't need to start with a book; start with a social media post, LinkedIn article, blog post, or video, and tell your story, a hero's journey, or the story of one of your employees, suppliers, friends, or even customers.

Storytelling in Sales: "Use storytelling to create an emotional connection with your audience. When you tell a story, you're not just selling a product or idea; you're selling an experience. For instance, instead of just listing the features of a product, share a story about how it improved someone's life."

Building Relationships: "Focus on building relationships rather than just closing deals. Long-term success in sales comes from cultivating trust and loyalty. This means following up with clients, being genuinely interested in their needs, and offering value even after the sale is made."

Active Listening: "Practice active listening. Instead of thinking about your next pitch while the other person is talking, truly listen to understand their needs and concerns. This builds rapport and helps you tailor your pitch to address their specific situation."

The Power of Questions: "Ask open-ended questions to engage your audience and uncover their true needs. Questions like 'Can you tell me more about your biggest challenge?' or 'What are your goals for the next quarter?' can reveal valuable insights that help you position your offering as the perfect solution."

Mindset and Attitude

Embrace Rejection: "Understand that rejection is part of the process. Every 'no' gets you closer to a 'yes.' Use rejection as a learning opportunity to refine your approach. Analyze what went wrong and how you can improve for the next opportunity."

Consistency and Persistence: "Consistency and persistence are key. Success in sales often comes from being the most consistent and persistent. Follow up regularly without being pushy, and keep refining your approach based on feedback and results."

Real-Life Examples and Anecdotes

Customer-Centric Approach: "Consider the story of how Nordstrom built its reputation on exceptional customer service. Their legendary approach to putting the customer first, such as accepting returns without question, has created a loyal customer base and a powerful brand identity."

Innovative Selling Techniques: "Highlight innovative selling techniques like social selling, where salespeople use social media to engage with potential customers, build relationships, and drive sales. Explain how platforms like LinkedIn can be leveraged to connect with prospects and share valuable content."

Tools and Resources

Utilizing Technology: "Leverage technology to enhance your sales process. Tools like CRM (Customer Relationship Management) systems can help you keep track of customer interactions, manage follow-ups, and analyze sales data to improve your strategies."

Training and Development: "Invest in continuous learning and development. Attend workshops, read books on sales strategies, and seek mentorship from experienced sales professionals. Continuous improvement keeps you sharp and adaptable in a constantly changing market."

Ethical Selling

Transparency and Honesty: "Promote transparency and honesty in all your sales interactions. Ethical selling builds trust and long-term relationships, which are more valuable than any single transaction. Never oversell or make promises you can't keep."

Customer Education: "Educate your customers. Instead of just selling a product, teach your customers how to make the best use of it. This not only helps them see the value in what you're offering but also positions you as a trusted advisor."

Incorporating these elements will make your chapter more comprehensive and valuable for your readers. It will provide them with practical tools and insights they can apply directly to their business and personal lives.

Steps to Effective Selling

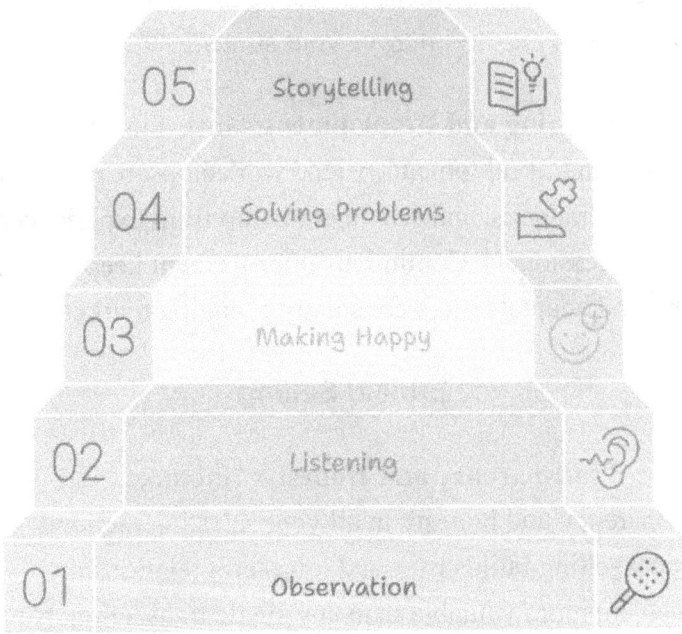

Figure 27 - Steps to Effective Selling

Chapter 27
Super-Networkers

Make Friends with Super-Networkers

"Super-Networkers will show you one of the best marketing karma strategies of all time!"

Super-Networkers are those people who happen to know a lot of people. They are popular, recognized, and respected. Whether it's in their nature to be sociable, or their family is well-known, or they have some connections, they are known in their job or charity organization. Imagine having not only one Super-Networker in your Rolodex but two, three, or twenty. You automatically have access to hundreds, even thousands, of people.

Super-Networkers aren't necessarily the winners of a popularity contest or the typical high school football captain or homecoming queen. They come in every shape and size. They could be politicians, published writers, or bloggers with a large following. Super-Networkers often have Marketing Karma that attracts others to them. They could be your friends or friends of your friends.

Finding and getting to know Super-Networkers is easy. Becoming one yourself is also possible. Learning to work with them and access their network is more challenging. You can't just walk in and ask them to call all their friends whenever you have a project, product, or event. Remember, you are promoting yourself, not just a project or product. You must help them promote themselves and be unselfish, and in turn, they will promote you to their friends, family, and whole network.

It doesn't matter if you're involved in a nonprofit function, promoting a product, or seeking investment for your company. Super-Networkers are the best for getting the word out. The key is how you work with them, approach them, and get them on your side. I remember a friend, a networker, who bought a new watch and wore it everywhere. It wasn't an expensive watch, but he loved it, and it looked great. He told all his friends about it, and soon, several of his friends bought the watch from the same retailer. He promoted it because he believed in the product. This is just one example of how Super-Networkers can help with your promotion.

When you think about Super-Networkers, you must think about both small and big. A few of them in your immediate circle can charge your promotion efforts quickly and effectively. A few high-profile Super-Networkers like actors, athletes, and politicians can supercharge your efforts. This is why companies pay them to wear their products and promote them in the media. Their circle of influence can reach around the world.

What Is a Super-Networker?

"A Super-Networker is a person who knows a lot of people and is liked, admired, and consulted."

A Super-Networker knows he receives good Karma when he refers you to a business in his network because he's helping you and the business.

Super-Networker Matrix

Access to one Super-Networker can introduce you to hundreds of people they know personally. The Super-Networker Matrix diagram illustrates how a Super-Networker might know different groups of people. One group could be friends from school, another could be acquaintances at a sporting club, or they might belong to a social club or other association. Don't think Alpha-Connectors have one big group of people they know and gather with all the time. More likely, they have different groups with different people.

In the diagram, Super-Connector 1, you see just the first part of what a larger matrix could be. The diagram shows the direct connections only, meaning people your Super-Networker knows directly. Each of those people knows at least one hundred others and has at least ten people in their immediate circle of influence. This means your promotion can reach thousands of people through the example of Super-Networkers. Get a couple of them on your side to promote, and you can easily reach tens of thousands of people.

This type of matrix can be very powerful. There are other considerations to the matrix you should learn before approaching it. Not all matrices are made of the same receptors or people. The people in the matrix have different interests, ages, and economic backgrounds. If you are looking for a matrix of students, you wouldn't approach your parents or grandparents to find Super-Networkers. You would contact young people, other students, class presidents, tutors, teachers, student associations, fraternities, sororities, clubs, and athletic departments.

Utilizing the Super-Networker Matrix

Use Matrices to promote yourself using Marketing Karma. Don't immediately push your products or services through your Super-Networker contacts because you will fail and, most importantly, burn a powerful matrix of thousands of people. If you push your company, product, or service from the start, they will see you as selfish, just a promoter. Don't be the "email spam" of promotions.

Once you establish your Matrices, you can use them effectively to promote yourself and your projects. Be creative and follow through with your promotions. For example, if you want to promote a specific project, cause, or product, you could print T-shirts about your project. Find Super-Networkers to wear the t-shirts, talk about them, or even wear them on their next Instagram post; the idea here is to ignite the matrix.

A great example is (PRODUCT) RED, a project Bono, the vocalist of the rock and U2, and Bobby Shriver started in 2006 to raise awareness and money for The Global Fund by teaming up with iconic brands to produce (PRODUCT) RED branded products. It's a Super-Networker Matrix put together like few can. Bono is the Super-Networker promoting the "Red" products, starting with t-shirts, cell phones, credit cards, iPods, and laptops. When you buy these items at participating retailers, a percentage of each (PRODUCT) RED product sold is given to The Global Fund, helping women and children affected by HIV/AIDS in Africa.

Can you imagine the matrix Bono created? Can you imagine the other Super-Networkers Bono knows or can reach? Numerous stars, including Julia Roberts, Penelope Cruz, and Natasha Bedingfield, promote the Red project. Oprah has promoted it on her TV show. Countless other rock stars, movie stars, and athletes are behind it.

Bono's Matrix isn't just about selling t-shirts or cell phones. It goes deeper. His goal is to help eliminate AIDS in Africa. This wonderful project started an educational movement teaching us that we can do something to help. When asked by Larry King why he got involved, Bono answered, "Someone needs to do something about it." That someone happens to be him. And he's extending the invitation to everyone in the developed world to participate in this change. The time is NOW.

The movement involves simple actions such as buying T-shirts, phones, shoes, and hats. He's proving that anyone can make a difference. Just by buying a product, you can save a life. This gets everyone involved, not just the United Nations or governments worldwide. It gets you and me involved in big, life-saving, world-saving projects. How's that for Bono's lesson on Marketing Karma? How's that for a matrix?

This T-shirt-buying, world-saving Matrix extends beyond Bono and Bobby Shriver. It taps into many other Super-Networker Matrices, like mine, influencing not just my friends and family but also my readers. My wife caught the Red bug, too. She bought Red products as gifts and asked her friends, "If you're buying me a birthday gift, I prefer Red." Furthermore, she educated her friends on why she only wanted Red and convinced them to give Red products for birthdays and Christmas for one year. How's that for a Matrix?

You can build your Networks using free tools that allow you to create groups of people with the same interests; for example, I like using X.com for their lists and communities, Discord, Telegraph, LinkedIn Groups, and Facebook Groups. You can also start or attend live events, expos, and mastermind groups. If you want to see if we have any open spots on our mastermind, contact my team at www.MastermindGroup.US.

Chapter 28
Advanced Marketing
Karma Strategies

In Chapter One, we explored the essence of Marketing Karma and Unselfish Self-Promotion—what it is, how it works, and why it works. We learned how to apply Marketing Karma to everyday life, ensuring we continue to know and understand ourselves and others long after finishing this book. Now, it's time to pull out the promotional toolbox, get to the fundamentals, and transform yourself into the brand manager you need to be.

Now that you have grasped the philosophy, strategy, and big picture of Marketing Karma and have pledged to follow the unselfish rules of self-promotion, you can apply real-world marketing and promotional strategies to promote yourself effectively.

We didn't start this book with these advanced techniques, such as internet marketing, public relations, or image management, because without understanding the principles of Marketing Karma, they won't work. Yes, you might see initial success since these are proven strategies, but without the "Karma" element, your results will falter and eventually fail.

These techniques will supercharge your promotion regardless of who you are or what you do—whether you're in business or not, a housewife or a CEO, a nonprofit visionary or a university student, a salesperson, or none of the above. These tools transcend your current occupation or job, social standing, and life stage. They adapt to who you are now and who you will become.

Here is a list of Advanced Promotional Tools to amplify your newfound promotional superpowers:

Advanced Promotional Tools

1. Search Engine Optimization (SEO)
2. Writing Articles for LinkedIn
3. Your Blog
4. Public Speaking
5. Business Cards
6. Shock & Awe Box
7. Writing Books
8. Press Releases
9. Social Media Videos and Posts
10. Whitepapers

Used together with sophisticated marketing plans, you can apply these superpowers to create funnels that will transform your life and your business. After you understand your personal brand, your UVP, USP, Avatar, and Promise, and your product and service, using them in funnels and tracking the results with simple mathematics will catapult

you, your company, and your products into the
stratosphere.

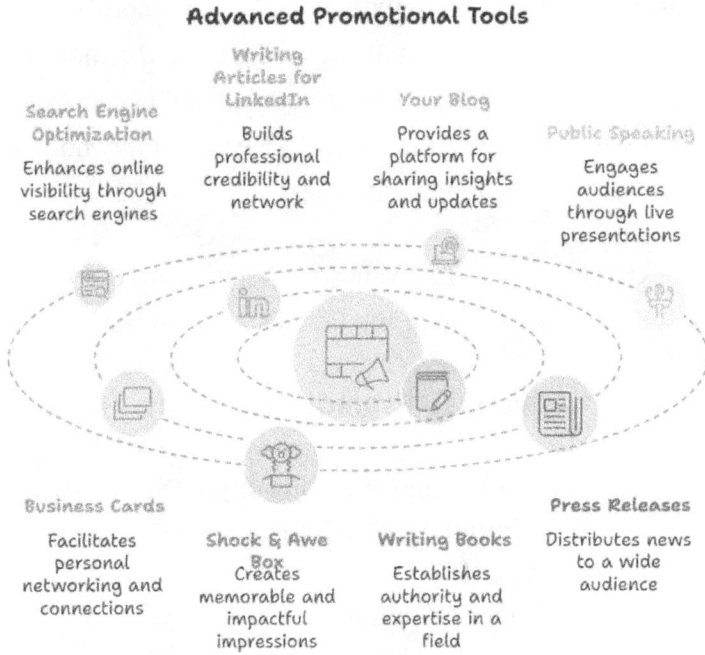

Advanced Promotional Tools

Writing
Articles for
LinkedIn

Search Engine
Optimization

Enhances online
visibility through
search engines

Builds
professional
credibility and
network

Your Blog

Provides a
platform for
sharing insights
and updates

Public Speaking

Engages
audiences
through live
presentations

Business Cards

Facilitates
personal
networking and
connections

Shock & Awe
Box
Creates
memorable and
impactful
impressions

Writing Books

Establishes
authority and
expertise in a
field

Press Releases

Distributes news
to a wide
audience

Figure 28 - Advanced Promotional Tools

Chapter 29
Digital Marketing

More Than Posting on Social Media

The internet is the great equalizer, and digital marketing is your secret weapon. Digital marketing encompasses email, SEO, blogs, social media, professional networks, text messaging, push notifications, online networks, phone networks, and other communication mediums you can use to spread your influence.

You can't get far in a marketing book without discussing digital marketing. I search online for books, services, restaurants, clothing, and almost everything else I want or need. As a marketing Vice President, Chief Marketing Officer, and entrepreneur, I've relied on digital marketing as the cornerstone of all my projects.

Digital marketing should be a significant part of your marketing plan. From videos to LinkedIn, Meta, TikTok, YouTube, email marketing, and Google advertising, testing and marketing online is easier and cheaper than traditional advertising like television, billboards, or printed magazines.

Digital marketing is going mainstream. You can now advertise on cable television directly from your computer, buy electronic billboard time, or run video ads on gas pumps or vending machines. One of my companies has six hundred vending machines with televisions, where we sell advertising to small and large consumer goods brands.

If you work for a company, you might use Microsoft Teams, Google Meet, or other project management and communication software. These tools also influence your personal brand. How you share, write, and conduct yourself within these tools contributes to your Marketing Karma.

Direct Response Marketing

"I love Direct Response Marketing."

Direct response marketing targets your ideal consumer directly, eliciting a response like a phone call or an email. It's measurable—you track every click, email, lead, prospect, sale, and upsell. In contrast, other marketing methods, such as trade shows or networking events, are harder to measure. That's why, before investing in a booth at an expo or trade show, I advise combining it with a direct marketing campaign to secure appointments during the event rather than relying on foot traffic.

Let's dive into how to combine your Digital Marketing Strategy with your Marketing Karma to achieve mind-blowing results!

Some of the tools you have in your Digital Direct Response Marketing could include:

- Traffic Magnet
- Lead Magnet
- Click Bate
- Squeeze Pages
- Thank You Pages
- Landing Pages
- Lead Ads
- Social Media Ads
- eBooks or Kindle Books
- SEO
- Email Autoresponders
- Live and Evergreen Webinars

All of your tools are useful. However, we also need to focus on developing a long-lasting campaign that brings you leads and customers not for a month but for a lifetime or at least five years. My favorite way of doing this is by writing a whitepaper, which is the click bate, traffic magnet, and lead magnet all in one, and using squeeze pages, landing pages, and email autoresponders to get emails, phone numbers, schedule video calls or webinars, and close sales.

Develop Your
Whitepaper Evergreen Funnel

When I started as a young marketing Vice President, the internet was new, Google wasn't around, and social media was just a dream. I was selling project management software to large companies and needed more leads. So, I built a simple funnel—a strategy I still use today.

The funnel was straightforward yet powerful. It started with a headline like "Project Management Software Whitepaper," aimed at decision-makers purchasing a new project management software system, which was a significant investment. The website was a squeeze page—a page designed to collect emails featuring a headline, a video, or minimal text, and a form for visitors to leave their name and email. After submitting their email, they'd be taken to a thank-you page to download the promised whitepaper.

After receiving the whitepaper, they'd get a series of emails from me with articles and information on project management software, culminating in an invitation for a live demonstration and a test user account.

This funnel still works today. During the pandemic, I used it to get customers for our white-label manufacturing programs, investors for various companies, and customers for my mentoring business, among other ventures.

Creating Your Evergreen Whitepaper Funnel

Here's what you need to develop your own evergreen whitepaper funnel:

- **Whitepaper:** At least ten pages long
- **Squeeze Page:** Collect names and emails
- **Thank You Page:** Deliver your whitepaper
- **Email Software:** Sequential autoresponder
- **Email Sequences:** Call to action
- **Traffic:** SEO, videos, ads, articles

Whether you're selling beverages, vitamins, software, or services or seeking investment, this funnel should be a must in your marketing toolbox.

Tools for Writing and Editing a White Paper

Creating a compelling white paper requires a blend of research, writing, and editing. Here are some essential tools to help you craft a high-quality white paper:

Research Tools

- **Google Scholar:** For finding scholarly articles and papers.
- **Statista:** For statistics and data.
- **JSTOR:** For accessing academic journals and books.

Writing Tools

- **Microsoft Word:** A robust tool for writing and formatting.
- **Google Docs:** Great for collaborative writing.
- **Scrivener:** Ideal for managing large writing projects and organizing research.

Editing Tools

- **Grammarly:** Helps with grammar, punctuation, and style.
- **Hemingway App:** Ensures your writing is clear and concise.
- **ProWritingAid:** Offers in-depth writing reports and style suggestions.
- **Readability Test Tool:** Checks the readability of your text.

Design Tools

- **Canva:** For creating visually appealing graphics and layouts.
- **Adobe InDesign:** Professional software for designing and formatting documents.
- **Visme:** For creating infographics and visual content.

The Power of the Internet

The internet is a place where anyone with access can find you. You can communicate with businesses and individuals, share information, collaborate, and send photos, brochures, articles, and videos.

Many understand the internet's power but don't fully grasp its potential. Here, you'll learn how to exploit the internet's potential. The internet is vast and multifaceted—a place to communicate, collaborate, and commercialize. I call this the internet's three C's.

The Internet's Three C's: Communicate, Collaborate, and Commercialize

The internet is more than just websites. Your potential for promotion isn't limited to your business or personal websites. You can write and publish articles for thousands of readers, send out free or inexpensive press releases, write eBooks, record audios, shoot photos and videos, and make them available to vast audiences—all for free.

The one thing that likely won't work is building a self-indulgent website and expecting thousands of visitors because you claim to have the best product or service. Having the "best" of anything isn't a unique selling proposition. Everyone claims to have the best because it's easy. It's not creative.

I work extensively with consumer goods, particularly beverages. Every month, about three hundred companies or individuals contact me about beverages. They all claim to have the best taste, package, or name. It's simple and not impressive. I'm waiting for someone to impress me with the best distribution, merchandising, or drop shipping sales program.

Let's not build a "self-indulgent, look at me" website. Let's establish our First Rule in Internet Marketing.

Digital Marketing Rule #1:
Don't Build a Self-Indulgent Website

You need to reveal who you are and what you do and convey details about your business, services, products, ideas, or nonprofit organizations—getting your voice heard and your message across is essential. The problem is that your message won't reach anyone without visitors or traffic. You might have the best-looking website, but if no one visits, it's useless.

One of my marketing consulting clients faced this issue. He invested $40,000 in a decent-looking website. He spent countless hours perfecting it and proudly showed it to everyone who visited his office. But those were the only visitors. Why? Because self-indulgent websites don't attract traffic. He was getting about twenty visitors per month, a poor result.

Why does this happen? The internet is content-based. Information rules, content is king, and value is the traffic magnet. You need to provide value to attract visitors.

We could spend chapters discussing Google algorithms and tweaking your website with keywords. Instead, let's focus on what your customer wants—what will keep leads and customers coming back for more—time after time.

Takeaway

Digital marketing is your secret weapon, the great equalizer that can elevate your brand and business. By understanding and applying these strategies—developing an evergreen whitepaper funnel, leveraging the internet's three C's, and avoiding self-indulgent websites—you'll harness the power of digital marketing to its fullest potential.

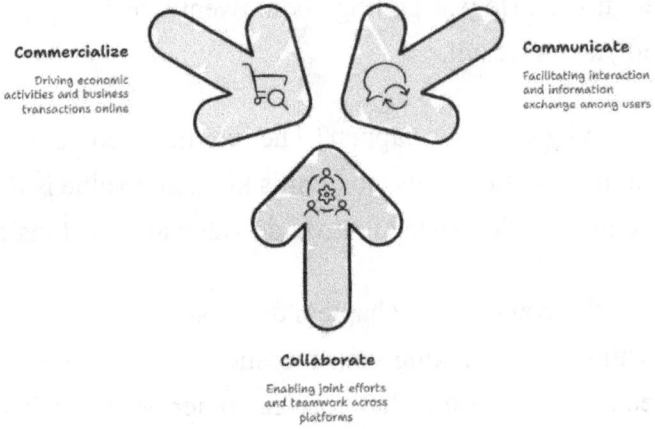

Figure 29 - The Internet's Three C's

Chapter 30
Traffic Magnets

A Traffic Magnet is an asset that attracts visitors to your site, like a well-written article with effective SEO. A Lead Magnet, on the other hand, is designed to capture leads—such as a whitepaper or webinar.

When people find your website through a Google search, that's a traffic magnet at work. If you create a LinkedIn article or TikTok video offering a free report, that's a lead magnet. These lead magnets might not always direct users to your website because social media platforms now offer Lead Forms. These forms allow you to deliver content, capture emails and phone numbers, and even sell products—all without leaving the platform.

Lead Magnets can include free reports, books, courses, or videos. We've discussed lead magnets in depth while working on your whitepaper campaign; now, let's focus on traffic magnets.

You might have noticed we haven't touched on your website structure yet. We haven't discussed how to build it, what to include, its appearance, or its design. We will cover those details soon, but first, we need to concentrate on something more crucial: driving traffic to your website, regardless of its current state.

The Secret to Attracting Traffic

So, how do you attract visitors? What's the trick? Actually, there is no trick, but there is a secret. Tricks are meant to deceive both people and search engines, and that's not effective. Tricks might work temporarily until search engines catch on and penalize you. Trust me, I've tried every trick in the book—and even wrote a book on them. It doesn't work. I've been penalized time and again. Deceiving visitors will only result in them leaving your site quickly once they realize there's no valuable information.

What you need to rank high in search engines, gain links, attract traffic, capture leads, and craft a stellar marketing strategy is value. Not just good prices or value-added sales but genuine value. This is the essence of Marketing Karma in digital marketing. Providing value through information, webinars, videos, articles, podcasts, research, advice, rules, techniques, templates, and even free chapters of your new book will yield Karma in the form of traffic, leads, and long-term customers.

Digital Marketing Rule #2 – Build Value

Let's break down how the internet works in terms of traffic, starting from step one. People go online to find information, be entertained, shop, conduct business, and more. They rarely look specifically for your company unless they have a business card, met you in person, or received a recommendation.

Knowing this, you need to provide what people are searching for: information, entertainment, collaboration, or commerce. The basic principles of Marketing Karma are even more applicable on the internet because they are faster and larger. People search for information quickly and will leave a webpage within seconds if they don't find what they need. You've experienced this yourself—searching for "internet marketing" and finding pages filled with sales pitches rather than useful information.

The internet's scale means you're not interacting with each visitor individually. You might receive thousands of visitors each month, far more than you could ever engage with personally. This is why the internet is bigger: it's accessible to a larger audience who can find and receive your tailored message.

Apply the same basic rules of Marketing Karma to your internet strategy and website development. See things from your visitor's perspective. Build your website to meet their needs and provide the information they seek.

Capturing Leads Through Value

Offering value doesn't mean giving everything away for free. You can use squeeze pages, landing pages, registration forms, and events to capture visitor information. This way, you turn visitors into leads. Once they are leads, you can provide more value to convert them into customers.

In my businesses, I always offer free information such as videos, audios, infographics, and articles. However, for the really valuable content—like hacks, templates, or high-value insights—I require registration. I usually ask for a name and email via a squeeze page or registration page.

A squeeze page is a short page that asks for the visitor's name and email in exchange for a free report, video, template, or other high-value information. If the visitor isn't willing to provide their information, they don't get the content. The squeeze page includes a headline, sub-headline, bullet points, a video, brief text, and an email capture form.

The headline and sub-headline promise something spectacular—not just the free report but the results it will bring. Bullet points highlight the transformations, benefits, features, and results. The text explains how they will get the information immediately after providing their name and email. The video reinforces these points and encourages immediate action.

Squeeze pages have been a standard for two decades and are used in every social media, online, or offline advertisement. For especially valuable information, I sometimes ask for a cell phone number. I don't make calls myself; instead, I use automated text software to deliver download instructions and follow up with texts for special events or exciting deals. Use texting sparingly and only for messages of significant value, such as giving away a new book.

The Key to Attracting Traffic

Figure 30 - The Key to Attracting Traffic

Chapter 31
Your Value-Based Website

Creating value is a cornerstone of Marketing Karma. Let's explore how I've created value in my companies and how you can do the same.

You need content—videos, audio, or written information- to create value. This takes time, but it could be the best use of your marketing efforts. With artificial intelligence and content repurposing tools, you can thrive on one good article per month, spinning it into LinkedIn articles and posts. In my company, we combine industry articles and news. For instance, if you seek funding, post information on investing and the latest investment news. I've applied this strategy across various industries, including beverages.

I've spent several years in the beverage industry, which is currently booming, especially in the "Functional Beverage" category, growing at 50% annually. Companies in this space are selling for billions, and valuations are soaring. The hot products over the past two decades included energy drinks, vitamin-infused water, ready-to-drink teas, tequila, and bourbon. The next big trends are

Delta 9 beverages, shots, mixers, and Mushroom-infused drinks. My partners and I own several beverage companies, R&D firms, and bottling plants in San Diego, CA. We've helped companies go public, manufactured for major brands, and assisted hundreds of entrepreneurs with courses, mentoring, R&D, manufacturing, and business modeling. How did we attract leads and establish ourselves in such a noisy market? Let's delve into how we create value for our customers.

Instead of creating a self-indulgent website that only showcases our company, we built a series of websites, each dedicated to a specific segment of the beverage industry, based on what people search for online. We created one site with free information on starting Delta 9 beverages, another on getting distributors, another on exporting to Mexico, and so forth.

What was the result? Thousands of newsletter subscribers and numerous requests for information, mentoring, manufacturing, business ventures, and partnerships—more than we ever imagined or could handle. This led to writing a book called "Build Your Beverage Empire," now in its third edition after two decades in print. The book answers ninety percent of questions a beverage entrepreneur might have, providing value to beverage entrepreneurs we couldn't personally assist. Offering free information is crucial, but reserving some content for marketing purposes and relationship-building is essential.

Following up with more information on your website is probably the most important aspect of your entire internet strategy. We'll cover this in detail in the upcoming chapters.

Building Your Valuable Traffic Magnet

Remember, by creating websites with useful information and content, people will find you. Search engines will love your site, ranking it high in search results. Gradually, you'll build a solid self-promotional machine—a traffic magnet.

From Zero to Traffic Magnet

It takes time to attract traffic. You need valuable content, lots of it if you don't have an advertising budget, or paid advertising if you do. You also need others to recognize your good content and link to your site. Search engines must see your valuable content. This combination builds a traffic magnet.

To attract organic traffic, provide relevant, non-self-indulgent information. Avoid focusing solely on sales pitches or product information. Offer real information—articles, case studies, how-to guides, research. If you're selling in your content, it's not traffic magnet material. This approach is one of the greatest promotions you'll do. You'll capture visitor information, keep them engaged with ongoing content, and convert them into customers, donors, voters, or whatever your goal may be.

Create new, exciting content for your website regularly. Start a blog, add videos, photos, and audio, and use all media types to provide value. The more varied your content—audio, video, photos—the more traffic you'll attract. Search engines will notice and reward you. Search engines aim to provide the best, most relevant information to their users. When you provide great information, you're partnering with search engines, making their job easier, and they'll send tons of traffic your way.

Capturing and Converting Traffic

Now that we understand the need for value and how to build traffic with it, we must capitalize on that traffic. Just because people visit your website doesn't mean they'll like you, buy from you, or believe your message. What's next? Marketing Karma will help you turn website or blog traffic into extreme promotion.

By focusing on creating value, you'll build a website that attracts, engages, and converts visitors, establishing a solid foundation for long-term success.

Chapter 32
Get Your Traffic Karma

When developing your value-based websites and blogs, imagine you are your own customer. What are their pain points? What are their goals? What information are they seeking, and how would they like to receive it? Use your buyer persona to identify keywords, questions, and solutions.

Google is an invaluable tool for discovering what your future clients are searching for. They'll likely Google questions or ask them on YouTube (owned by Google) and even TikTok if your target market is younger. In Google, search for the key terms your clients might use, such as "beverage formulation" or "beverage manufacturing." Google will return a mix of ads, videos, and questions. Focus on the videos and the questions—they reveal what your target market is asking and watching. To create value, answer these questions in a video and then repurpose the video transcript into a blog article on your website.

Recently, there's been a shift from traditional websites to social media accounts and pages. Use these platforms—LinkedIn, Facebook, TikTok, and Instagram—as you would use your website. They allow for medium-length articles and engaging posts. However, don't substitute your website entirely with these platforms. Why? Because you need to own the analytics, leads, and traffic. Develop a loyal following that willingly shares their email and phone number with you.

Maintain your Amazon store, TikTok shop, and other forms of communication and sales, but also sell your products and services on your own website. This way, you own the supply chain, which increases your valuation.

As a writer of children's books, business guides, self-growth, history, investing, sociopolitical, and even fantasy and science fiction, I started selling eBooks twenty-five years ago. I stopped relying solely on Amazon.com and traditional book distributors.

People surfing the internet seek value, information, and entertainment. As a promoter, you should focus on the Internet's three C's: Collaboration, Communication, and Commercialization. This section will guide you in building your internet strategy around these core principles.

Your Core Strategy: Websites, Mailing Lists, and Content

Your Core Strategy includes three fundamental elements for a supercharged internet presence: your websites, mailing list, and content.

Other strategies exist to attract visitors to your website, but it's pointless to draw them in if you're not ready to capitalize on their interest. It's like throwing marketing money away. Prepare yourself for the traffic, leads, questions, and search engines. Your Internet Core Strategy ensures you're ready for all of this.

One quick way to prepare for traffic is by capturing emails using a whitepaper lead magnet, for example. Direct visitors to a squeeze page to collect their email, enroll them in your email autoresponder, show them a video on the thank you page, and invite them to book an appointment with you in that video. During this appointment, you can sell your products and services.

Core Strategy Elements

Websites
Essential for establishing your online presence.

Mailing List
Crucial for direct communication with your audience.

Content
Key to engaging and retaining visitors.

Figure 31 - Core Strategy Elements

Chapter 33
Your Outfacing
Personal Brand

Image Is Everything

Imagine you're at a reunion with friends or colleagues. People are seated, standing, talking, drinking wine, laughing, and socializing. You walk into the room, and someone says, "Wow, you have a fine-looking suit," or "That's a nice shirt."

Does this happen to you often? If not, you might be skeptical about this chapter. But by the end, you'll be a believer. We just need to understand your image bias.

I love wearing jeans and T-shirts. In sunny San Diego, I take it further, often donning my favorite pair of huaraches, summer linen pants, and a T-shirt. It's my personality, my life, and my fashion. Or is it?

You should feel comfortable with what you wear and how you look—not just your clothing, but your body too. This doesn't mean you should ignore or neglect your appearance. Quite the opposite, you need to be fully aware of how you look, dress, and feel. The way you communicate with others is crucial for self-promotion, and YOU are the first thing you're communicating: your appearance, smell, dress, walk, posture, smile, speech, and interactions. You can't promote yourself effectively if you can't do it in person. Your image is the cornerstone of "In-Person Self-Promotion."

Your appearance matters, and it encompasses more than just your clothes. It includes your car, house, glasses, watch, haircut, skin—everything. This also involves your social interaction skills, posture, and style.

Some may argue these things shouldn't matter; maybe people should have "Heart X-Ray" glasses to see your true nature. I agree; this is an ideal. But in reality, not everyone perceives the world this way. To draw people in and let them see who you truly are, you need a good image at all times.

Fake It Till You Make It!

When I was broke, I bought used Italian shoes and restored them. I hunted for dress shirts under $10, and I had one pair of black dress pants. It was enough to land me my first big job.

You don't have to be rich to look clean and professional. But you do need to look presentable and maybe even develop your own personal style. Don't be afraid of being different, funky, or kooky.

Did You Shine Your Shoes Today?

At a business dinner in Houston with an executive from a large Pennsylvania company, I observed something interesting. He wore a shiny suit and tie with slicked-back hair. As a VP of Business Development, I had already applied many Marketing Karma strategies, so I observed him closely. Despite his claims of rapid career advancement and success, his appearance didn't match his words. His suit looked cheap, his watch and pen seemed fake, and his shoes were unpolished.

Why did I doubt him? His appearance. I had no other reference, just that conversation and his image. He seemed like a slick salesperson, which made me wary of his authenticity. His suit's fabric and cut, his fake Rolex, and his neglected shoes all screamed insincerity.

The lesson? If you want to feel like a million bucks and be perceived as such, you need to look the part. I'm not saying you should buy a fancy watch or custom suit, but at least shine your shoes!

Looking good at all times is crucial. Pay attention to your clothing, car, accessories, hair, nails, hands, face, shoes, and briefcase. The goal isn't to spend extravagantly but to be presentable.

When it comes to clothing and accessories, stick to your budget but think critically about your choices. It's not about the cost but the fit, cleanliness, and style. Start with easy fixes like shining your shoes, cutting your nails, styling your hair, and ensuring your clothes are clean, pressed, and matching. Then, move to more challenging aspects like staying in shape or being the best-dressed.

You Are Your Own Brand Manager

Imagine having a team: a talent agent, publicist, personal lawyer, accountant, trainer, nutritionist, cook, and image manager. You'd be like a movie star or professional athlete. You need to take on this role yourself because you have your best interests at heart.

Your Brand Manager ensures you stay healthy, in shape, and happy, maintaining your relationships and image. Be your own Brand Manager.

Dress for Success

Remember, it's not about being trendy; it's about looking good. Here's some practical advice to help you look better:

- Always wear clean clothes; discard anything torn. Keep the ripped jeans, but don't wear them to work.
- Polish your shoes. Carry a small polisher in your briefcase, car, or suitcase.
- Brush your teeth three times a day. Carry a toothbrush and dental floss in your purse or briefcase.
- Keep your nails clean. Carry a nail clipper.
- Mind your hair. Ask for advice from friends, a spouse, or a hairstylist.
- Keep facial hair in check. Either shave or keep it trimmed and neat.
- Iron your clothes.
- Match your belt and suit. Black shoes require a black belt; brown shoes need a brown belt.
- Buy quality, stylish shoes. People notice shoes and judge attention to detail.
- Invest in shoes before shirts and pants.
- Match socks to pants if you're conservative; wear funky socks if you're not. I do both!
- Ensure clothes fit properly. Avoid pants that are too long.
- If you wear glasses, keep them clean. They're a window into who you are.
- Tone down cologne for work.
- No socks with sandals. If you wear open-toed sandals, keep your feet groomed.
- Keep your car clean inside and out.
- Get in shape. People admire those who are in good shape.

Components of Professional Appearance

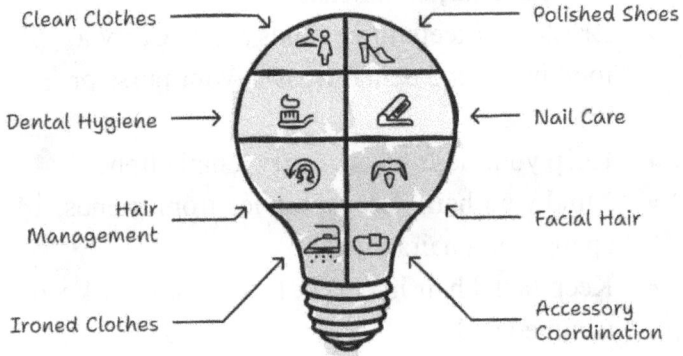

Clean Clothes

Polished Shoes

Dental Hygiene

Nail Care

Hair Management

Facial Hair

Ironed Clothes

Accessory Coordination

Figure 32 - Dress for Success Guidelines

Conclusion

As we reach the conclusion of "Marketing Karma," it is essential to reflect on the journey we have undertaken together. This book is not merely a collection of marketing strategies but a transformative guide that bridges the gap between professional success and personal fulfillment. By embracing the principles of Marketing Karma, you are embarking on a path that promises sustainable growth, meaningful relationships, and a deeply satisfying life.

The Essence of Marketing Karma

Marketing Karma is built on the foundational belief that your actions have a direct and profound impact on your outcomes. It is the practice of promoting yourself, your products, and your services with an unselfish mindset, always prioritizing the well-being and success of others. This approach not only fosters goodwill but also creates a positive ripple effect that returns to you in the form of trust, loyalty, and opportunities.

Throughout this book, we have explored various laws of Marketing Karma, each offering unique insights and actionable strategies. From the Law of Cause and Effect to the Law of Giving and Hospitality, these principles guide you in cultivating a magnetic personality and a compelling brand that resonates with your audience.

Practical Application in Business and Life

One of the most significant takeaways from this journey is the realization that Marketing Karma is not confined to the business realm. It extends to every aspect of your life, influencing how you interact with family, friends, colleagues, and even strangers. By adopting a mindset of unselfish promotion, you create an environment where positive energy thrives, attracting success and happiness naturally.

In business, Marketing Karma translates to ethical marketing practices, genuine customer engagement, and the creation of value-driven content. Whether you are a seasoned entrepreneur or just starting, these strategies will help you build a robust brand that stands the test of time. In your personal life, applying Marketing Karma means nurturing relationships, being present in the moment, and continuously striving for personal growth.

The Long-Term Vision

The concept of Big Picture Promotion underscores the importance of thinking long-term. Your promotional efforts should not be short-sighted or solely focused on immediate gains. Instead, envision your brand's legacy and work towards creating a lasting impact. This involves consistently aligning your actions with your core values, investing in meaningful relationships, and continuously learning and adapting.

As you navigate through various projects, businesses, and life stages, maintaining a Big Picture mindset ensures that your efforts contribute to a larger purpose. This approach not only enhances your personal and professional growth but also positions you as a thought leader and an influential figure in your community.

Embracing Change and Growth

Change is an inevitable part of life and business. The Law of Change reminds us that growth requires adaptability and a willingness to embrace new opportunities. By staying open to change, you can continuously evolve and innovate, keeping your brand relevant and dynamic.

Marketing Karma encourages you to view challenges as opportunities for growth. Each obstacle you encounter is a chance to refine your strategies, learn new skills, and strengthen your resilience. This proactive mindset will enable you to navigate uncertainties with confidence and emerge stronger.

The Power of Authenticity

In a world where authenticity is often overshadowed by superficiality, Marketing Karma stands out as a beacon of genuine connection. Authenticity is not just about being true to yourself but also about being transparent and honest in your interactions. It builds trust, fosters loyalty, and creates a sense of belonging among your audience.

As you implement the principles of Marketing Karma, remember that authenticity is your most valuable asset. Let your true self shine through in your promotions, communications, and everyday actions. This authenticity will resonate deeply with those around you, creating lasting and meaningful connections.

The Journey Ahead

The journey of Marketing Karma does not end with this book. It is an ongoing process of self-discovery, growth, and purposeful action. As you continue to apply these principles, you will witness the transformative power of unselfish promotion in your life and business.

Keep in mind that success is not measured solely by financial gains or professional accolades. True success encompasses personal fulfillment, positive relationships, and a sense of purpose. By integrating Marketing Karma into your daily life, you are not only paving the way for your own success but also contributing to the well-being and happiness of those around you.

Final Thoughts

In conclusion, "Marketing Karma" offers a comprehensive roadmap to achieving success through unselfish promotion. By embracing the laws of Marketing Karma, you can create a powerful and positive impact on your life and business. Remember, the essence of Marketing Karma lies in the simple yet profound principle of giving more than you receive. As you move forward, let this guiding philosophy shape your actions, decisions, and interactions.

Thank you for embarking on this journey with me. May the principles of Marketing Karma lead you to a future filled with success, happiness, and fulfillment.

Table of Figures

Index

U

W

Y

www.ingramcontent.com/pod-product-compliance
Lightning Source LLC
Chambersburg PA
CBHW060324200326
41519CB00011BA/1830